ENERGETIC AWAKENING

Rev. Scott Beebe

World Thoughts Publishing
St. Augustine, Fl.

Energetic Awakening
World Thoughts/2001

The information contained within this book reflects the personal experience of the author and the people that have participated in the spiritual growth process described. It is not intended as a replacement for accepted medical practice, although it is believed that if used as a supplement, healing can be greatly accelerated. If you are in the care of a Physician, always first consult with your doctor before suspending any treatment or medication.

All rights are reserved.
Copyright © 2001 by Scott Beebe
Cover picture by Robert Blaize
CD copyright © 2001 by Robert Blaize

No part of this book may be reproduced or transmitted in any form or by any means, electronic or mechanical, including photocopies, recording, or by any information storage or retrieval system, without permission in writing from the author or the publisher.

Address:
World Thoughts
P.O. Box 3206
St. Augustine, Fl. 32084-3206

beebes@aug.com
www.WorldThoughts.com
www.energeticawakening.com

ISBN 0-9711018-7-6

How To Use This Book

A tool is an instrument we use to aid us in performing a task. Without a specific tool, many tasks and operations would be very difficult, if not impossible, to accomplish. This book is a tool to aid you in the task of spiritual growth. Every good tool has a correct application to achieve the desired results, so I will explain how this one works.

The first half of the book is the vehicle for change and transformation. It is important that you start at the very beginning, because the opening and clearing of the Heart Chakra is essential to the subsequent releasing process. The opening of the heart chakra will initiate clearing and release of energetic blockages in your core energy body. The seven steps described in Part I, will help you remove blockages from the emotional, mental and spiritual bodies, as well as realign these subtle bodies. Everyone needs help in one or more of these areas. That is why you are here on Earth in a physical body. It was faulty perception that brought you here and only correct perception will allow you to leave. The affirmation exercises at the beginning of each section will focus your intent and energy toward accomplishing the desired result. The subsequent information provided will allow you to form a mental image of what is happening on an energetic level.

As the energy body clears and is readjusted, it is also important that you learn to balance your energy. This means that you spend time every day

Energetic Awakening

centering yourself at your heart chakra. Meditation, prayer and yoga are all wonderful techniques that will accomplish this. The CD, which is included with this book, is an excellent tool to aid you in balancing your energy. Listen to it often! Balancing your energy on a regular basis will help you keep the release out of the physical.

Follow your intuition as to how much time you need to spend in each section and the time to be spent between sections. Move as quickly as you feel comfortable with, but not too quickly, or your release may seem overwhelming.

The second part of the book describes my journey that led me to this information. Everyone has a journey and this is mine. Use this part of the book to break up the sections in part I. Although I tell my story chronlogically, it doesn't matter where you choose to read here.

Table of Contents

Part I - Transformation

	Page
Step 1: Opening the Heart Chakra	1
Step 2: Clearing the Emotional Body	17
Step 3: Clearing the Mental Body	25
Step 4: Clearing the Spiritual Body	28
Step 5: Realigning the Emotional Body	32
Step 6: Realigning the Mental Body	37
Step 7: Realigning the Spiritual Body	38
Advanced Energetics	39

Part II - The Journey

Balance and Harmony	53
Karma	63
Guidance	71
Asia	82
Lessons	89
Onslaught	97
Recovery	103
Compassion	113
Case Histories	119
Maps	137
Bibliography	139

Acknowledgments

I would like to especially thank my wife, Sigi, and my two daughters, Zara and Miria, for their support and understanding during the trying times in my spiritual unfolding. I am certain that we were all brought together to support each other in our growth.

I would also like to thank the many people who have expressed interest and support in the completion of this book. It is my hope that we will all grow to the full expression of our soul.

Finally, would like to acknowledge and thank the founders of the New Horizons Church, Rev. Diane and Rev. Michael Parks-Isam, for their support and guidance in my spiritual development.

Energetic Awakening

Part I

Transformation

Energetic Awakening

Introduction

This book will stimulate profound change in you. It is a book to promote spiritual growth, from which everything else originates. The growth that you will experience is a result of your willingness to grow and the focusing of your intent to release all low frequency blockages that you have created. These blockages include not only what you have created in this lifetime, but also in all previous existences you have experienced. You create blockages when you think at variance with universal law, which is love. Every thought you think creates a thought form, or energy field that has a particular frequency and shape. The more your thought is in accordance with principles of love, the higher its frequency and more balanced the thought form. Thoughts that deviate from this truth, such as thoughts of anger, hate, fear and jealousy, create low frequency thought forms that are distorted and lodge in your energy field as energetic blockages. These blockages are then mirrored or manifested in your physical condition, both internally as exhibited by your physical health and externally in the events that happen to you in your life. The main focus of intent will be the clearing of blockage and the restoration of your energy body to its pure and unblemished state.

Step 1: Opening and Clearing Your Heart Chakra

Place your hand on your heart chakra, in the middle of your chest. Focus your intent on your heart chakra and visualize it opening. Now imagine a beam of high frequency energy pouring into the heart chakra and breaking up any low frequency patterns it encounters. Your heart chakra is now open and clear!

You are an energy being that your senses tell you is a physical body. If you could adjust your senses to see the energy body, and the energy bodies that surround you, the world would appear completely different. Who are you as an energy being? What would it look like to see your energy body? Fibers of light are interlaced throughout all levels of the energy body as well as the physical body. Energy blockages create areas of murkiness, becoming even black in areas were the energy no longer penetrates. The fewer blockages you have accumulated, the brighter you appear. You constantly interact with the energy fields of the people and objects around you. Every thought you have about someone or something sends a connecting light fiber. Distance has no meaning here, and these connecting fibers can reach around the world in an instant. Everything affects your energy field. The colors you wear, your jewelry, your perfume or cologne, the food you eat and the relationships you have all interact with you. You live in a sea of energy!

Everything is interconnected; everything is inseparable.

Let me introduce you to yourself. Imagine yourself as a being of light, encased in a cocoon of light that extends outward from your center. The body is energy in its dense, particle form. Extending outward is layer upon layer of structured energy, which some refer to as the aura. The first energy layer beyond your physical body is the Astral Body. It is tied into all areas of your physical body. The astral body remains when you die and drop your physical body. It extends out from your physical body about two inches and then merges into the finer energy layer referred to as the Emotional Body. Your emotional body is directly tied into your heart, circulatory system, and nervous system. Emotional stress primarily affects these systems. Extending outward to approximately six inches, your emotional body continues into your Mental Body. The mental body, about 10 inches from the physical body, is where the process of thought is carried out. It is linked directly to the brain and endocrine system. Finally, beyond the mental body, there is your Spiritual Body. The spiritual body extends to two feet and beyond. The spiritual body is your link to the angelic realm, the universe, and ultimately God.

Two primary energy matrixes connect your physical body with your energy body. The first matrix is called the acupuncture system. It consists of acupuncture meridians and acupuncture points. These energy pathways are interwoven with the physical, emotional, mental, and spiritual bodies. The activation of acupuncture points stimulates the flow of energy at all levels. The second matrix is the Chakra System.

There are seven primary chakras and numerous secondary chakras or light centers, connected with your physical body. The first primary chakra is located at the coccyx, at the base of your spine and is also referred to as the Root Chakra. The second chakra is just above the pubic bone. The solar plexus is the site of the third chakra. The heart chakra is on the midline of the body, just above the end of the sternum. The fifth chakra, or communication center, is at the base of the throat. The sixth is in the center of the forehead. It is referred to as the brow or third eye chakra. The seventh, or crown chakra, is on the top of the head. Beyond the seven chakra centers, are five others that extend into your energy body. The eighth, located about 6 inches over the head, is in the emotional body and is also your access to the angelic realm. The ninth, in the mental body, is about 10 inches over the head and is the seat for soul development. The 10th, 11th and 12 chakras are found in different levels of the spiritual body.

Your cells, tissues, organs, and organ systems, as well as your aural layers, all need a balanced supply of energy. This is furnished through the acupuncture meridian and chakra energy pathways. This energy consists of the Yin and Yang energies. Yin is the female, negatively charged, dark, cool, receptive, nurturing, and fertile energy. Yang is the male, positively charged, creative, hot, light energy. The interplay between these two determines the cosmic dance of all life and matter in the universe. Acupuncture meridians supply the yin and the chakra system furnishes the yang. Some organs require higher amounts of yin energy and are referred to as yin organs, like the kidneys and heart. Yang organs include the intestines and stomach. All of your organs however, need both energies in sufficient amounts. Blockages or restrictions in the energy flow lead to imbalance and eventually to sickness.

The intake of energy is initially through the heart chakra. It is then distributed throughout your energy body to all other areas. Energy blockages at the heart restrict the amount of energy available, thereby reducing the overall energy flow to the entire body. Most religions emphasize the necessity of having a "pure", unencumbered heart. True forgiveness removes heart blockages and allows the yin and yang energies to flow freely along the energy pathways. The body is the extension of the aura. All blockages originate in your aural layers and find manifestation in your body. Your biology is your biography! (Myss)

Stress is the cause of all energetic imbalances. It is the causative force whose symptoms are sickness, aging, and death. Stress originates in both the emotional and mental bodies, but primarily in the mental body. Every thought you have creates an energy field. These fields contain both yin and yang energies, depending on the focus of the thought. Each energy field also has a particular vibrational rate or frequency to which it resonates. Thoughts of love, unity and happiness create high frequency fields and thoughts of anger, hate, sadness and depression generate lower frequency fields. The high frequency patterns pass freely out along the spiritual body, while low vibrational forms lodge in your energetic pathways in much the same way as cholesterol clogs the veins and arteries of your circulatory system. With time, these fields restrict the flow of energy to your cells. Severe restriction results in disease conditions.

Sin is the name we give in religion to stress. To sin is to have thoughts in discord with the universal principles of love. Every sin creates stress and a low frequency energy field, which restricts your flow of energy. To be without sin is to be completely stress free! No sin is greater than another. The difference is the area in which it lodges in your energy body. Those sins that are most detrimental to you locate in your heart area. The "moral sins", outlined in the Ten Commandments, restrict the energy flow to the heart chakra, thereby affecting the entire body. The mechanism of forgiveness removes these blockages. Most religions use forgiveness as a tool to spiritual growth. All forms of stress, whether physical, emotional, mental or even spiritual, block energy flow at some level. Sin originates in the mental body and the low frequency energy field is already in place by the time the thought translates into action. That is why Jesus said that you have already sinned with the thought. The action is merely the manifestation of the low vibrational thought into the physical level.

Fear, in all of its forms, is stress. Sin and fear result from faulty perception. Fear can be a positive force to help you to avoid potentially dangerous situations, but for the most part, fear is detrimental in your life. You create fear within your mind, or it would not exist. It varies in degree from mild anxiety to paralyzing terror, but always creates a low frequency energy field. These fields block and restrict the energy flow through your mental, emotional, and physical bodies.

You have developed different stress reducing strategies in your life. Some are conscious strategies, but many occur unconsciously. Sickness is one of the most notable of the unconscious strategies. You may have difficulty viewing sickness in its positive form, but becoming ill is a major release of low frequency blockages. If you do not consciously and continuously rid yourself of stress, nature will lend you a helping hand. When you are sick, you step outside your normal patterns of life and take a break from your routines. Some sickness can be quite debilitating, attacking you where stress is most pronounced. Stress weakens your immune system, which opens your physical body to a variety of diseases. If the blockages cannot be removed from the energy body, other symptoms will develop.

Dreaming is another method you employ to reduce stress. When you dream, you directly involve the mental and emotional bodies. Generally, this is carried out on an unconscious level. Psychology uses dream interpretation to zero in on the areas of the mental body where energy channels are clogged by low frequency "memories" and bring them to a conscious level where they can be recognized and perhaps resolved.

Conscious stress reducing strategies include playing a sport, exercising, Yoga, meditation, prayer, and hobbies. Each area has its own particular effectiveness to open up the energy channels. Conscious stress reduction is by far the most effective and least painful path to take!

Chances are that your heart chakra has some energy blockage. Over 99% of all people that I energy-chart have heart chakra blockage. With few exceptions, only young children through to the age of 6 to 7 years old are clear. At this age, the mental body can begin to create thought forms and low frequency energy fields will block the heart chakra. Extensive blockage leads to heart disease. Faulty perception is always the source of blockage. Once the blockage is removed, it is important that it is not re-created through a current situation. One of the main perceptions that create heart blockage is that of being hurt or victimized by someone. This blockage will remain until you release all feelings of resentment, and forgive. Nothing can threaten that which is real. Misperceiving this creates fear, resentment and self-pity. Keeping the heart chakra open and clear is essential to continued spiritual growth!

High frequency energy entering your heart chakra will force low frequency blockage to vibrate loose and surface. As your blockage surfaces, you will re-experience it in some form, depending on what the blockage is. You may find yourself getting angry or irritated for no obvious reason, or experience some fear or sadness you had stored away.

Keeping your energy balanced will allow the release to continue at an accelerated rate and keep it out of the physical. There are many techniques to balance your energy. If you practice meditation, yoga, or prayer, you already have a balancing technique. The meditation CD included with this book is designed to balance your energy. Rigorous exercise is also a good way to release and balance. Focus on your heart chakra while you are balancing. Swimming in salt water is great for breaking up the surfacing low frequency patterns. Sea salt from a local health food store will also help you release. Add water to about ¼ cup of sea salt and rub it on your skin before you shower, making sure you scrub the bottoms of your feet and the palms of your hands. All of these techniques will assist you to stay balanced and ease the releasing process.

As you release blockage, your vibrational frequency increases at every chakra level. You are in essence becoming lighter. The more and the faster you release, the brighter you become as stress falls away from you. It is not a good time to make any life changing decisions, because the release will cloud your perception of what the issues are. Just stay balanced and aware of what is happening around you.

Energy is everywhere, and it has structure. It is also non-local, which means it can be accessed from anywhere in the world. Energy follows thought, so if you think of someone, no matter where he is, you are immediately connected to him energetically. This connection is much more than some whimsical fantasy; it is real!

All blockages and the resulting karma it creates are the result of misunderstanding and misperceiving who we are in relation to everything else. The stress that causes energy blockages originates in the mental body, and is caused by faulty perception. Your stress is based on the failure to answer three basic questions: "Where did I come from?" "Where am I going?" and, "What am I supposed to do in the meantime?" These questions are what you try to resolve in one form or another during your whole lifetime. Unfortunately, you have very little idea of who you are or what anything is. You are limited by your five senses, and your senses provide your image of the world.

From the moment you exit the womb, you begin gathering sensory data about yourself and the world around you. Your brain at first perceives the world as a kaleidoscope of movement, color, and indiscernible forms. Soon you are able to isolate differences in your environment into shapes, sounds, and objects. Neurons connect in your nervous system to create neural pathways. As a child develops, more and more "free" neurons are committed to electrical pathways until, by the age of six, the main circuitry is already established. Further learning proceeds as an unfolding of pathways already formed.

You learn experientially. Knowledge falls into two categories, knowledge by acquaintance, or knowledge by description. Knowledge by acquaintance includes what you learn that can't be explained, like the color red, a sunrise, or how to ride a bike. Knowledge by description is everything you know, and can communicate. This includes the facts and concepts you generally refer to as knowledge. As your accumulation of data increases, you form a hierarchy of information, which forms the bases for your extension of knowledge.

This web of beliefs becomes your view of the world. At the core of this web are your basic assumptions about reality. Faulty perception at the core is analogous to building your house on sand instead of rock. New information is rejected if not harmonious, or integrated if congruent. People are usually very resistant to internal or external change. Occasionally, you must radically alter your beliefs. Emotional, mental, or physical suffering is your feedback system to monitor perception.

Buddhism describes three principle pathways out of suffering, and all three involve techniques to alter the way you view reality. If you see the world as a fearful, dangerous place, then that is how it will eventually appear to you. If you view the world as a beautiful, wondrous, loving place, then that is what you will perceive wherever you look.

Let's examine your basic assumption of separateness. This assumption relies on your senses that tell you that the world is composed of different objects and life forms, and that you are separate and distinct. As stated before, your brain learns to divide forms according to similarities and differences, and assigns specific characteristics to each. Both physicists and mystics will tell you that, in reality, there are only superficial divisions between objects and that everything is interconnected. At the sub-atomic level, there are no objects. Atoms interact freely with surrounding atoms and establish patterns of relationships. Isn't that what you establish in your life, patterns of relationships? Everything is interconnected, and the degree to which you recognize this determines correct perception.

Examine another of your perceptions: Time. You see time as a continuum, moving from the past, through the present, and into the future. Your observations and memory seem to support this hypothesis, but does time really exist? The only moment you can truly know is *now*. But, even as your brain recognizes *now*, it is already gone. *Now* is a state of being beyond thought. What you think of as *now* is really only second-hand news. The past only exists as a reconstruction of what you perceived as a previous *now*. The future exists only as a probability in your mind. Time, with its chronology and incremental units is a construct, a tool you use. It appears to exist, but has no meaning when applied to the infinite.

Space is another concept you consider basic. Science and logic tell you that no two objects can occupy the same space at the same time. Again, physics has shown that there are no solid objects. What you consider objects are made of atoms, which are mostly empty space. Matter can be converted to energy, and energy to matter. Space becomes a relative concept. There are many dimensions superimposed on our own, unseen and undetected by us, but occupying the same "space". There are vast regions of empty space, not only between atoms, but within atoms, as well. You observe the same sort of pattern as you expand your perception into outer space. Vast regions of empty space separating regions of material density. The activity and diversity you perceive at this level is the exception.

Your senses are useful for operating in the world, but only present a small portion of what exists. The narrow range of light wavelengths your eyes can register limits vision. The mid-sonic range at which your eardrums vibrate limits sound. Lower or higher vibrations cannot be seen or heard without technical assistance. Touch is registered by the firing of neurons, which only fire at certain threshold levels of stimulation. The ability to sense smell and taste are much reduced, compared to other animals. Your "window" of reality is extremely small in relation to what exists.

The brain, that marvelous instrument, filters through vast amounts of sensory data, searching for patterns with which it is familiar. Information is filtered out if it doesn't fit into established patterns of prior knowledge. Your subconscious, or unconscious mind records what your senses perceive, but most of it never surfaces. Instruments, including the microscope and telescope have extended your natural senses, but have only slightly expanded your "window". You still only see what you are looking for. It is like being in a box of mirrors, you continually see your own self reflected back wherever you look.

Limited ranges of sensory perception, together with incomplete understanding of what there is to understand, form the basis of your fundamental assumptions. Understanding yourself and everything in your world is constructed on the foundation of your core assumptions. If these are faulty, then everything you think you understand contains a degree of error. The truth is, that you know nothing for sure! Faulty perception is what causes stress; correct perception is what releases it.

Everyone learns biases, prejudices, and faulty belief systems that, once accepted, hinder a more complete understanding. We all maintain we want to know the truth, but we constantly limit ourselves in its acquisition. Organized religion can severely limit understanding. Each religion purports to have discovered the "truth", which remains exclusive to them alone.

What is correct perception and how do you achieve it? First of all, correct perception is not "truth", but it is as close as you can get to it within the existing limitations. Through the ages, the main tenets of religion have acted as beacons to light our way to correct perception. Most religions provide for some form of accountability. Your actions and thoughts have a weight or value attached to them that determine what your afterlife conditions will be. Another concept inherent in all religions is unity. "Love your neighbor as yourself" can be expanded to all life and to all things in the universe.

 "Maya", or the illusion projected by your senses is an eastern philosophy. Western belief systems also recognize sensory limitations to explain some experiences by requiring faith. Reincarnation has broad based support in eastern belief systems, but is bitterly opposed in Christianity. Present decisions determine everlasting Heaven or Hell.

The Buddhists describe 104 different astral levels of existence beyond the physical. The lower astral levels correspond with the Christian version of Hell, but are subdivided into the seven hot and seven cold Hells, the temporary Hell, the intermittent Hell, etc. The worst version of Hell is the Vajra Hell, or the place of everlasting darkness, where you wander alone forever. Above the Hells are the lower and middle Heavens. These areas are more pleasant, but you are still working off previous lifetime "debts". The upper Heavens, for advanced souls, are described as glorious places, each with its own perks. The quantity of sins and indiscretions you have committed in a life, determines the weight of your soul. The heavier you are, the further you sink down. Likewise, the lighter you are, the higher you ascend. Returning to this plane of existence gives you another opportunity to better your position by absolving negative karma. Which perception do we choose? All systems are mutually exclusive. Which belief system has correct perception? All of them do, but none of them are true!

Let me present a metaphor that is also not true, but is close to correct perception. Imagine all of humanity as a single developing organism, a fetus in the egg of the Earth. Starting from only two sex cells, male and female, fertilization occurs, and cells begin multiplying. The developing embryo grows and eventually, specialization occurs. Individual cells activate portions of their DNA, according to a master genetic plan. Parallels can easily be seen here with Adam and Eve, and with the emergence of different populations and cultures. The Bible refers to the tower of Babel, where all of mankind spoke a single language and strived to rival the Gods. At this point, God sent confusion into their minds, so each spoke a different language and went in separate directions. Specialization had occurred. As humanity continued to grow and specialize in this metaphorical embryo, different organs began to emerge, composed of specialized groups of tissues, but all according to the DNA blueprint. The growing organism, although very small initially, later grows exponentially in mass and cell number. The living and dying of people also parallel the cell processes of the body. Eventually, as the fetus continues to develop, distinct groups of cells become functioning organs; the nervous system and the brain, the heart and the circulatory system, the liver, spleen, pancreas, etc. Each organ is composed of a distinct specialized tissue, or groups of tissues, that all begin functioning according to their specific characteristics. Buddhism, dealing with the development of the mind, would represent the brain and the nervous system. Christianity, with Jesus, represents the heart and the circulatory system. Missionaries expand the veins, arteries, and capillaries throughout the organism. Moslems represent the liver and digestive system. The liver purges and detoxifies the system, as well as providing bile (oil) to aid in the digestion process. As growth increases, so does the amount of waste produced, to the point where the fetus is in danger of poisoning itself with its own waste products. Sound familiar? In the later stages of its development, the systems of the organism begin to work in harmony and unison with each other to integrate all aspects of the body. The new life is ready to emerge from the egg.

Envision the shell of the egg as our ozone atmosphere, which is slowly showing signs of "cracking" at the poles. The ozone holes are getting larger and larger as the egg begins to hatch. Will this organism, called Mankind, be ready to emerge? Will its systems integrate in time to support its continued development? Will people of various religions realize that they are all part of a unified whole, unfolding according to a master encoded plan? A body does not only consist of a heart or a brain or a liver, but each is an integral part of the whole. The complete organism cannot survive without them. This is correct perception!

Step 2: Clearing Blockages from Your Emotional Body

Focus your intent once again at the heart chakra. Expand your awareness out to include your emotional body, about six inches from your physical. Now ask for all major blockages to be removed. Direct your focus and breath to every chakra, starting with the Root Chakra and working upwards through the 12th, breathing the blockage out as you focus intent.

Since 1998, there has been a tremendous shift of consciousness and energy on this planet. The Yin, or female energy, has expanded and increased steadily in frequency. At first it was slow, only one unit a month, but then accelerated, until it was increasing a unit each day. It reached 222 Yin units on May 3rd of 1999. At this threshold, the Earth went into an exponential acceleration. I refer to it as the infinite. This was also the day that Oklahoma experienced some of the worst tornadoes in its history. The tornado is a spiral energy, or yin energy. The yang, or heavenly energy, also increased dramatically during this period. This increase gives rise to a tremendous potential for developing consciousness and increasing vibrational frequency.

To better understand the mechanics of blockage, I want to relate a truth, "As Inside, So Outside". Your perception of the external world is a mirroring of your internal world. Personal problems and crisis situations you experience in the world around you are the symptoms of a blocked energy flow within your energy body. This applies to physical problems, as well. The physical body reflects and manifests the energy body restrictions. The symptoms of energy blockages are also the blockages in your life. Financial problems, sexual problems, relationship problems; the list goes on and on. The problems cannot be solved by constantly addressing the symptoms! Energy blockage is the problem and there it must be solved. Leaving a relationship, moving to a new location, and taking medication only temporarily alleviate the symptoms.

Psychological therapies attempt to isolate the situation that caused the blockage, but do not eliminate the resultant energy blockage. They superficially address faulty perception. Faulty perception causes stress, stress produces energy blockages, and these blockages are mirrored in your interaction with the physical world. Karmic blockages present a further difficulty for a psychologist. Children who are born with defects, or contract severe diseases at an early age already have energy blockages in place before birth. These generate situations in their lifetime that reflect the blockages. Not considering past life experiences severely limits the ability to access the root cause. But energy is energy, and all blockages can be removed at an energy level, past or present.

I want to speak now of the work that I do charting people's energy, detecting blockage in the different bodies and, most important, the removal of those blockages. Most of the charting is done at a distance, via telephone. We are all unified at a higher level, so I can access an individual's Higher Self to obtain the information I need. I use the pendulum as my tool. The rotational direction of the pendulum indicates a "yes" or "no", in response to the questions I ask.

When charting your energy, I first ask how many of your chakras are open. Everyone uses nine chakras, which extend from the root chakra at the base of the spine to the ninth chakra, over your head. The first seven chakras connect directly to the physical body, the eighth is the access to the angelic realm and the ninth deals with soul development. Some people also have the tenth, eleventh, or the twelfth open, which are all located in the spiritual body.

I then chart the distribution of your energy at each of the open chakras. Each chakra manages a portion of the total energy you take in. The tenth through twelfth chakras require no input of energy on your part and can give you additional energy to work with.

The next aspect of the chakras, with which I'm concerned, is the vibrational frequency of the yin and yang energy. I compare your yin frequency units with those of the Earth's. There is a direct correlation of these values to the functioning of the immune system. A low frequency at any particular chakra, points to a genetic condition. The top three chakras do not apply to the physical. The yang frequency shows me the extent of blockage in the energy body. This value is compared to the frequency you would have if the energy body were completely cleared of blockage. The difference between the two values represents your total blockage in the core energy body.

Energetic Awakening

I chart the consciousness level you were born into, and where you are presently. These levels are expressed as different colored "rays. The lowest ray is red, for the root chakra. I have never charted anyone at that level. Red would indicate a low consciousness, Neanderthal-like individual. This ray has all but disappeared from the Earth. The next ray is orange, representing the second chakra. As with the red ray, this consciousness level is almost extinct. Choices you make in your lifetime determine your level. Yellow is the next ray level, representing the solar plexus, or third chakra. There are still many people at this level. It is the "warrior energy", and people here can be found throughout the military of all nations. The fourth consciousness level is the green ray, representing the heart chakra. Green is the healing color. Many people at this level find their way into the medical profession. The blue, or throat chakra ray, is the next level. People at this consciousness level use communication as a tool, such as teachers, diplomats, and social workers. The violet ray has become predominant in children born after 1975. Individuals at this consciousness level are well advanced. Many are in leadership positions, counseling, and the ministry.

The crown chakra ray, or the indigo ray, is the level to which many newborns are now entering this life. This level is very advanced for the Earth and indicates a significant energy-shift taking place. Indigo ray individuals often enter occupations involving the counseling and care of children. Beyond these seven rays is the white, or eighth chakra ray. These people are rare. A person born at the white ray consciousness level has come on a mission to serve humanity. They have brought no karma to resolve, and have volunteered to incarnate on the physical level out of compassion for others. They might include spiritual teachers, Holy Men, and Saints. The next ray, which I have only charted three times, is the gold ray, or the soul chakra ray. They have returned to serve, but in a larger perspective. To my knowledge, no one has ever entered a physical body on Earth at a higher level. After gold, the next level is the platinum, or tenth ray. We are now moving into the spectrum of the spiritual body. The eleventh ray is the diamond ray, and the twelfth is the emerald ray, or Christ/ Buddha consciousness. There are people, who have progressed to high levels in their lifetime on Earth. Names like Jesus, Mohammed, and Siddh Hartha come to mind immediately. They have left their mark on humanity long after their physical death.

Once I establish a base-line chart, I inquire into the blockages that you have. The most important of these is heart chakra blockage. The heart is the key! All energy enters through the heart chakra. If the heart is blocked, it can greatly reduce the total amount of energy you have to work with. Opening the heart chakra allows the energy to again flow freely and ends separateness. The most common blockage occurs in the yin or yang aspects of the emotional or mental bodies. Blockage in the spiritual body only occurs if you are being interfered with by low frequency entities. This is rare, but does occur. In these cases, I would insist that the entities leave you to continue their own evolution.

With the heart chakra open and unobstructed and the

other blockages removed, the process toward enlightenment proceeds. Enlightenment is the process of becoming lighter, or filled with light. Increased movement of energy through the energy body reflects an immediate change in the energy chart. The increase affects all chakra levels, but especially the yang frequencies.

The yang frequencies move through a series of steps to an accumulative value of over 22,200 units. As you move through the steps, levels of your energy body clear of blockage. The clearing proceeds from the astral body outwards to the spiritual body. At 22,200, you reach the Emerald ray, or Christ consciousness ray. At this point, your energy goes infinite. Having passed through this barrier, there is no falling back. You will never fall to the lower ray levels again. You are like an infant in the infinite. You will continue growing and expanding now forever!

Boils appeared on the back of my legs in my own release. I was informed that it was the residue of childhood sicknesses that were patterned at a cellular level. Also, the backs of my legs and buttocks became very sore and tender for about a week. This was the patterning of spankings I had received as a child. Other people experience release according to their individual patterning. Remember that you are moving out stress and heaviness that you have carried your entire lifetime.

Again, keep the heart chakra clear! Unless the heart chakra is unobstructed, there will be no progress. To have a "pure" heart means forgiving; forgiving yourself and others. It means inviting spiritual guidance into your life and following your heart. To follow your head is to move in circles. Logic only reflects itself, and is always inconclusive. A clean heart is the only directional compass to follow. Once you have moved your energy through the last barrier, you are in a position to help others.

With your core energy body cleared, your gifts become more apparent and unfold. If you are an intuitive, you may perceive auditory communication taking place with your spiritual advisors. It becomes easier to separate your thoughts from those of your guides as you progress energetically. A visionary may become aware of the spiritual realm by seeing it with eyes closed. A prophet may begin to experience visions of future events. Whatever your gift, it will develop further. Who knows what potentials you have slumbering within?

Enlightenment is different from what you may have imagined. Enlightenment means you are filled with light. There is no more darkness within. It does not mean that you walk about in constant bliss. You still have your personality, your quirks, and your habits. You still have your established patterns of thought and emotions. Love and compassion become the guiding factors of your life. You feel a desire to help and encourage other human beings to also become complete. Everything becomes clearer. Your corrected perception takes you above the battlefield of life, and you glimpse the bigger picture. You realize that everyone in your life has been a helper and supporter in your journey to completion. Those who have helped the most were those you found most annoying or difficult. They have provided you with the motivation to change. All resentment disappears as you realize this, and it is replaced by gratitude and love. The world is no longer a fearful place, and you are no longer a victim. And this is just the beginning!

Step 3: Clearing Blockages from Your Mental Body

You live in a world of ideas. These ideas are based in part on the interpretation of sensory data from your body. Your brain organizes the arrangement of this data into patterns of relationships. At the center of this process is your consciousness of self.

Focus your intent once again at the heart chakra. Expand your awareness out to include your mental body, about ten inches from your physical. Now ask for all major blockages to be removed. Direct your focus and breath to every chakra, starting with the Root Chakra and working upwards through the 12th, breathing the blockage out as you focus intent.

It is safe to say that no two people in the world perceive everything in exactly the same way. Each builds his or her "web of beliefs" on learned and self-generated assumptions. Everything you hold to be true is supported by other things you hold to be true. This chain of reasoning is always based on assumptions. You no longer question something you consider "true". Conflicting concepts force you to review your existing belief system. You can accommodate new information if there is not substantial conflict. If the conflict is too painful, you reject the new information. Conflicting ideas generally cause some discomfort.

If you were happy and content, why would you want to change?

If each person's perception of reality differs from everyone else's, whose is correct? Obviously, no one's is. At the core of each person's reality is his or her awareness of self. Surrounding that, are your "a priori" assumptions that form the basis for everything else. These beliefs are so deep and fundamental that you rarely question them. To question them is too painful. It would mean that you would then question everything you believe, because these fundamental concepts are your world. But, it is exactly in these areas that deep energy blockage occurs!

Examine the fundamental concept of self. Where some people identify self with a physical body, others maintain you are an eternal soul. Some believe you are born as a lowly sinner and will always remain so unless you accept their version of the "truth". Others believe in a long journey of progressive lifetimes, where the self can develop and unfold into the infinite. Your image of self can vary between low and despicable to high and pure. You have no empirical basis for either assumption. What you believe determines how you perceive your life and everyone around you.

Truth does exist in this world of relativism. Truth is one and unified. To grasp a part is to see the whole. Correct perception is the road to truth. Thoughts, concepts, and beliefs that block energy flow are faulty perception. This statement is based on experience, and experience is undeniable. You may not be clear on the what, why, and wherefore, but experience itself is basic. Raw sensory data embodies correct perception. It is the interpretation of this data that leads us astray. You experience energy all of the time, but your brain filters parts of that sensory information out. It is considered unimportant and non-essential for your survival. You can reprogram your brain to allow that sensory information to surface into your conscious mind.

I developed energy receptivity as I began to consciously search out the acupuncture and chakra points of the Earth. It was as though I had an antenna that could register this energy. I experienced it as a slight, directional pressure in my head. I felt dizziness when on a point, comparable to a moderate intake of alcohol. My gift is that of a "feeler", which means that I process information primarily through my seventh chakra, or the mind. I also have an exaggerated attunement to the "feel" of things. Everyone has this ability, although not always consciously.

My web of beliefs shifted as I began to assimilate and integrate conflicting information and concepts. I expanded the parameters of what I thought was true and possible, to include a wider range of observable and experiential phenomena. I tried to keep an open mind when confronted with new information. Like pieces in a puzzle, it began to fall into place and make sense. Those pressing questions, mentioned earlier, found answers.

Step 4: Clearing Blockages from Your Spiritual Body

Blockage in the spiritual body is rare and is always an indication that a spiritual entity has attached itself to your energy body. These attachments can range from a slight interaction to a full-fledged possession. Multiple personality disorders are examples of the latter. This is not allowed under spiritual law, but some entities choose this avenue for release as opposed to incarnating again into the physical. We are continually returning, because blockage can only be released in the physical. Inmates of prisons and asylums may hold many such attachments. Important to remember is that these entities are stuck at this plane of existence and are usually more than willing to carry on in their own evolution if they can be shown the way. You can become the bridge that helps them in their own spiritual progress.

Focus your intent at the heart chakra. Extend your awareness to include your spiritual body, about eighteen inches from your physical. Now call your Guides. Ask your highest spiritual archetype to escort any attachments you may have to another realm.

Spiritual Body

Perceiving yourself correctly will aid you in understanding another truth, "As Above, so Below". This means that everything, from the smallest to the largest, mirrors everything else.

The Earth is a spiritual being, undergoing its own release and participating in its own spiritual evolution. As a spiritual Being, it has an energy body consisting of aural levels, a meridian system and a chakra system. Under its crust, the physical Earth has energy alignments that parallel your own organ system (see map 1 at the end of the book). Earth meridian systems have long been speculated. The Chinese use the term "Dragon Lines" to describe the movement of energy along invisible pathways on the planet's surface. Alfred Watkins coined the term "Ley Lines" for energy channels that appear to connect ancient holy sites in Great Britain. The Earth's meridian-chakra systems extend over the entire planet. The chakras appear as spirals when mapped, in much the same way as our own. They rotate either clockwise or counterclockwise, depending on whether energy is spiraling up from or down into the Earth.

From atoms to galaxies, nature uses variations on the same fundamental pattern in every size and scale of the creation. This basic pattern involves the relationship between the two energies, yin and yang, and their unification to form universal energy. The physical manifestation of this pattern is expressed in what we call the Golden Mean. The Greek letter "Phi" represents the Golden Mean or the Divine Proportion. The simplest expression of the Golden Mean is the division of a line with any given length into a small part and a large part. The relationship of the small length of the line to the large length is in the same proportion as the relationship of the large length of the line to the whole. These three unequal parts (small part, large part, whole line) are proportionally similar. The only proportion that produces an unequal division that retains essential unity is the relationship of 1 to 1.61803….. The size or shape of the whole defines the size or shape of the parts. The small part is a scale model of the large part and the large part is a scale model of the whole. The number of the Golden Mean is produced entirely from the number 1 interacting with itself. This is illustrated by the following mathematical expressions of Phi:

$$\Phi = 1 + \cfrac{1}{1 + \cfrac{1}{1 + \cfrac{1}{1 + \cfrac{1}{1 + \cdots}}}}$$

$$\Phi = \sqrt{1 + \sqrt{1 + \sqrt{1 + \sqrt{1 \cdot \sqrt{\cdots}}}}}$$

The Golden relationship is an expression of unity, a unity pattern, because each part is defined completely by its relationship to the whole.

This relationship is evidenced throughout the natural world. The curvature of the ram's horn and the nautilus shell show the spiral of the Golden Arc, which is derived from the Golden Mean. The Golden Arc also describes the curvature of a wave or the eye of a hurricane. The relationship between your finger-joint to the adjacent one, of your finger to the hand, of the hand to the arm, etc., all approximate the Golden Mean. The proportions of insects and fish, the distribution of the leaves around the stem of a plant for maximum exposure to light can all be derived from Phi. The distance from Mercury to Venus is approximately 1.61803 times the distance of the sun to Mercury and the distance from Earth to Mars is approximately 1.61803 times the distance from Venus to Earth. Even the DNA helix mirrors the Golden Mean. One complete revolution of the DNA double helix measures 34 angstroms (an angstrom is one-billionth of a meter). The width of the DNA helix is 21 angstroms. The ratio 34:21 is approximately the Golden Mean (McIntosh). All reality mirrors itself. We were created in the image of God.

Step 5: Re-aligning Your Emotional Body

Energy flows from one aural level to another. A misalignment in the emotional, mental or spiritual bodies will restrict the flow of energy and create blockage. A misalignment is a distortion or a warping in the energy field caused by prolonged adherence to faulty perception or by tramatic relationship experiences. Often, these misalignments are already present at birth. Trauma affects the emotional body and prolonged misperception affects the mental body.

Focus your awareness on your heart chakra. Now close your eyes and envision yourself. Intend that your Emotional Body becomes re-aligned. Ask Spirit for it to be re-aligned.

Removing blockages and re-aligning the subtle bodies, effectively alters perception. Otherwise, you are constantly running up against patterns already in place. What you observe in your life reflects your blockage, whether health problems or life problems. Correct perception should be your goal. All misperception is deviation from the principles of love.

We need to understand the lessons of karma, blockages and misalignments. They are there for a reason and the reason is always the same. You would be amazed at the extent of your being. Once you have moved your frequency beyond the 22,200 yang unit

Emotional Re-alignment

threshold, you have cleared your core energy body. That is, however, only the first big step. It is a necessary step for further spiritual growth. With your core energy body clear and your heart chakra open and clear, you begin releasing from your extended light body, or your "Merchur". The merchur extends out to 55 feet in diameter around us. Karmic patterns of your human lifetimes on Earth are stored here. You brought a piece of this "mountain of karma" in with you to work on, when you incarnated into this lifetime. The rest stayed in the extended light body.

Although more elliptical in nature, I chart the merchur like a cube. This is not a truly accurate representation of this layer of your energy body, but it serves to illustrate the clearing that needs to be done. The cube consists of twelve positions or layers on the vertical axis, twelve on the horizontal axis and twelve in the depth: 12x12x12, or 1728 positions. Each position represents karmic patterns we need to release. Release proceeds naturally as an extension of the core energy body clearing. Charting reveals the extent of the clearing accomplished and also allows you to focus on areas that have not yet opened. Bach Flower essences from your local health food store aid in the process, especially essences such as crabapple or olive. Allow yourself to be guided to the essence best suited to your situation. The core energy body takes three to four months to clear once the major blockages have been removed. The extended light body can take six or more months. Not really long considering all of the lifetimes it has taken to accumulate.

You are at a unique time in your evolution as a soul. The Earth is going through its own evolution in frequency acceleration. The acceleration of the Earth frequencies forces a reciprocal clearing in us. We have little choice in this matter. We are on the brink of a massive releasing and clearing for the population of the Earth! This as a necessary step in our evolution, but it also means stress. Consciously focusing on your own release helps the mass of humanity to move forward.

Once the extended light-body clears, you access the Earth Body. This level is as large as the Earth and includes karma in forms other than human. This level takes about six months to clear. The release takes place predominately through the heart chakra. Beyond the Earth Body, you have the Solar System Body. This clearing relates to karma you have accrued on other planets in the solar system. The planet Venus is the site of most of those experiences. To clear this body takes six to twelve months. Your Galactic Body borders your Solar System Body. This level includes the karma you have created in other solar systems in the Milky Way. The Galactic Body may also take a year to clear. Finally, your Universal Body contains the karma from other galaxies you have inhabited and encompasses the entire universe. You are clearing back to the Source; releasing back to the first misperception; back to the first deviation from LOVE. You are the total of Creation. You are the image of everything that exists. Your soul has existed since the foundation of the universe!

You are a part of everything and everything is a part of you. We are all subsets of one. This individuality together with unity is the mystery of Phi and the mystery of the Trinity. It is important to realize that we are all interconnected during the process of releasing. You are constantly releasing for others as well as yourself. We are in a sea of energy, and energy exchange is a natural occurrence. You are an instrument of release for those around you and those that enter your thoughts. Become aware of when you are releasing for others. Although it is a compassionate gesture, your release for others does not appreciably help them. They will replace those blockages that you clear for them with new blockage. Unless their hearts are open, their major blockages removed and the subtle bodies aligned, your release for them will have served no purpose.

Releasing for others often involves physical symptoms. Initially, it is difficult to differentiate your own release from that of others, but as your frequency increases you soon learn to separate the two. Clogging up of the sinuses, body aches, sudden strong release through the heart chakra, or sudden allergy-like symptoms are all indicators of release for others. It is necessary to first realize that it is happening, before you can detach yourself from their release. Intend to detach and mentally step back from whomever you are releasing for. This will break off the energetic connection and relieve the physical symptoms.

This cannot be done when you have formed an energetic unit with someone. A unit is formed when you make a vow before Spirit to be with that person. One does not have to marry, although typically, a unit is formed in marriage. Your energy merges with theirs at a soul level. Both energies are tied to each other and move as one. Each partner in the unit releases for the other. It is advisable to chart both partners when I energy-chart people in a unit. Little progress is accomplished if I clear one set of blockages and not the other. Your conscious choice to end a relationship does not necessarily break a unit. Once formed, only your Higher Self can break a unit. A unit is also broken when a new one is formed. Your unit partner is, literally, your "soul mate".

Step 6: Re-aligning Your Mental Body

The mental body is where we store blockages created by judgments we have made concerning others. When you judge others, you misperceive who they are. Prolonged misperception can create a distortion or a warping in the mental body. This distortion does not allow energy to move freely between the subtle bodies. Restrictions reduce the amount of energy that is able to flow. A misalignment of the mental body affects the emotional body and the physical body.

Focus your awareness on your heart chakra. Now close your eyes and envision yourself. Intend that your Mental Body becomes re-aligned. Ask Spirit for it to be re-aligned.

Spiritual growth is a force within you. It is the knowledge of your perfection and divinity. The only thing standing in the way is what you have created. Everyone is doing the best that they can do. To grow spiritually is the awareness that everything is spiritual. This awareness may presently only be a dawning in your mind, but later, it becomes a certainty. Reality is much more than your five senses reveal. You can also interact with reality on other levels of awareness. Losing all fear of the afterlife and of death, you will feel as comfortable as you do in the world created by your senses. Love becomes your operating principle when fear no longer dictates your choices. You are on the road of correct perception. It will lead you to truth and truth will set you free.

Step 7: Spiritual Body Misalignment

Spiritual body misalignment, as with spiritual blockage, is rare. It is formed when you have been involved in occult activity in this lifetime or previously. In particular, it is the result of inviting low frequency entities into your life for the purposes of power. A distortion or warping in your spiritual body is caused by this misdirection of spiritual energy. It restricts the flow of energy to the mental, emotional and physical bodies. You have probably brought it into this lifetime as a karmic pattern and have been carrying it for many lifetimes. Search your heart.

Focus your awareness on your heart chakra. Now close your eyes and envision yourself. Intend that your Spiritual Body becomes re-aligned. Ask Spirit for it to be re-aligned.

You have cleared yourself now of all major blockage and misalignments of your core energy body. Remember that the most important focus now is balance. The enclosed CD is a helpful tool to achieve this goal. Blocking your heart chakra will shut down the process. Always be forgiving, especially to yourself. Repeat the process of unblocking and re-alignment if you feel your heart has closed or that you have created some other major blockage. All you need is the desire to grow and Spirit will provide the rest. Enjoy the journey of your life!

Advanced Energetics

Clearing the Core Energy Body is the first all-important step on your process of spiritual growth. This layer of your energy, extending out to about two feet around you, holds the patterns you have created in this lifetime, plus those karmic patterns you brought in with you to work on. To clear these blockages, your heart chakra must be open, your emotional, mental and spiritual bodies must be clear of blockage and aligned, and you need to have moved your vibrational frequency over 22,200 Yang units of energy. Achieving this frequency means that you have released all of the low frequency patterns within your Core Energy Body. It then seals, which prevents future blockage from accumulating again. The previous chapters of Energetic Awakening have outlined this process to you.

Beyond the Core Energy Body, you have the Extended Light Body, or the Merchur. This level of your energy extends out to a radius of about fifty-five feet in all directions from your physical body. The Merchur holds all of the karmic patterns we have created in our previous lifetimes as a human on Earth. These patterns are reflected in your present life experiences in both your physical well-being and in your relationships. The karmic patterns are charted by their position in your energy field. I chart this energy level like a three dimensional cube. This representation of your Extended Light Body serves as a model to enable me to record your progress and also to identify the nature of the blockage. Each axis of this cube contains twelve positions, or 12 x 12 x 12 = 1728 positions containing karmic patterns. The patterns arrange themselves in layers of a particular frequency. I am including several of these charts and case histories at the end of the book.

I have also identified vibrational keys, which can assist you in opening specific layers that are resistant to release. These vibrational keys are stones and crystals that correspond to the twelve stones in the breastplate of Aaron, described in the Bible in Exodus (28:15 – 28:30). The purpose of Aaron wearing the breastplate in the presence of God was to have the energy body as "clean" as possible. Some of the stones mentioned in the Bible have been substituted, but the vibrational effect has remained the same. Carry them with you or wear these stones as jewelry to have them assist you in opening and clearing a particular layer. The following is a list of the karmic patterns in each of the twelve layers and the vibrational keys that assist in their release.

Extended Light Body

Layer	Karmic Pattern	Vibrational Key
12	Parents	Chrysoprase
11	Earth	Beryl
10	Environment (Plants & Animals)	Jade
9	Fear of Rejection	GreenGarnet
8	Authority	Quartz, (smoky)
7	Guides	Blue Sapphire
6	Fear of Disease	Amethyst
5	Partner	Lapis
4	Fear of Death	Emerald
3	Children	Golden Topaz
2	Siblings	Carnelian
1	Humanity	Red Garnet

Notice that the list contains not only relationship issues, but also your fears. Your fear of rejection, of disease and of death, give rise to all the other worries and anxieties you experience in your life. All karma is created due to your perception of separateness. This misperception is maintained and perpetuated in all aspects of your relationships. At a sub-atomic level, there are no objects, only patterns of relationships without distinct borders or divisions. This is also true at every level of existence. We see ourselves as separate and distinct from everything else. This creates patterns of separateness between what we perceive as "me" and "them" (or it). These low frequency patterns give rise to fears, which also become patterns. The release of these patterns in our energy layers ends separateness.

Let us examine the layers of the Extended Light Body, to better understand the nature of the blockages we have created. These layers do not match up with the twelve chakras charted in the Core Energy Body. This is a different level of energy. Layer twelve deals with your relationship to your parents. It is important to keep in mind that these patterns were created in other lifetimes and are only reflected in this life. Those people you consider to be your parents have contracted to provide you with experiences in this life, which will bring your blockages to the surface. This allows you the opportunity to heal and release them. Your inability to do this will result in the repetition of these patterns in lifetime after lifetime, until they are released. In essence, everyone you have relationships with is attempting to help you grow spiritually. The patterns located in the 12th layer deal with your feelings of not being loved unconditionally by your parents. Not being understood, protected or supported, are all perceptions that can lead to blockages. Think of those issues that would be the most difficult for you to talk about with your parents and those are the patterns that need releasing. In some cases, it may be necessary for you to speak to your parents, especially if your parents are still living and these issues are a part of your current reality. If it is impossible to talk to your parents, for whatever reason, call them to you in Spirit and tell them what you feel. All healing comes from forgiveness; you forgiving them and yourself for any perceived injustices. These patterns will usually be released naturally if you have not experienced any negative reinforcement in your present life. Chrysoprase is the vibrational key for the 12th layer.

Layer eleven deals with your relationship to the Earth. The Earth needs to be supported, cherished and respected. Many earlier cultures realized this and maintained a close affinity to the Earth and the earth processes. Your lack of this awareness in previous lifetimes accounts for your blockages in the 11th layer. Beryl is the vibrational key for the 11th layer.

The 10th layer deals with your relationship to all life on Earth. The patterns are similar to the previous layer, but apply directly to the many life forms inhabiting the planet. Lack of respect and disassociation from plants and animals, except as a food source, gave rise to blockages in the 10th layer. Again, keep in mind that these blockages originated in previous existences and may or may not be reflected in this one. Green Jade is the vibrational key for this layer.

The 9th layer holds patterns of your fear of

rejection. Rejection implies separateness and loss of love. This fear stems from your misperception that rejection is even possible. Recalling those feelings and forgiving the people and yourself will help to release these patterns. Green Garnet is the vibrational key for the 9th layer.

The 8th layer contains low frequency patterns towards people in authority positions. This may be reflected in your relationship to your parents, your boss or anyone else you perceive having authority over you. These patterns involve feelings of resentment, fear, rebelliousness and disrespect. To release these patterns, you must realize that the only control another person has over you is what you have given them! You must speak your truth. The realization that your perceived adversary is also your supporter will help you to clear these blockages. Smokey Quartz is the vibrational key for the 8th layer.

The seventh layer concerns your relationship to your spiritual Guides. Everyone has spiritual Guides or what some call "Guardian Angels", assigned to them. These Guides are there to assist us in our process of spiritual growth. They communicate to us through our intuition as well as our thoughts. Everyone has them, although their assignments may change as you grow and progress on your spiritual path. Not trusting or acting on your intuition is what cuts you off from your Guides. Having faith and trusting your inner voice is what opens the communication channels to your Guides and releases the blockage patterns located in the 7th layer. Blue Sapphire is the vibrational key for the 7th layer.

The sixth layer contains patterns concerning your fear of disease. Illness always serves the purpose of releasing energetic blockage patterns. Getting sick is not a matter of being at the wrong place at the wrong time, but is a mechanism that your spirit employs to help you grow spiritually, because you are not listening otherwise. Sickness is the symptom of the low frequency energy patterns, not the problem itself! Core Energy Body blockage may manifest in some illnesses, but many diseases result from patterns within the Extended Light Body. The origin of others may be in your subsequent energy levels, which I will describe later. Clearing the blockage patterns in your energy field will result in sickness becoming unnecessary. The fear of disease can often only be overcome by confronting the situation. The vibrational key for the 6th layer is Amethyst.

Partner karma is found in the 5th layer. These issues concern distrust, disrespect, negative judgment, control and lack of acceptance. This relates to a life partner, not a business partner, unless your business partner is your life partner as well. All of these issues are reflected at times in a normal partnership and our ability to heal and release these patterns determines the depth and integrity of our relationship. Your partner can be most helpful to you in releasing and healing your low frequency patterns. Lapis Lazuli is the vibrational key for partnerships.

Layer four holds patterns of your fear of death. Many of your deaths have been traumatic. You have created patterns of fear as a result. To release your fear of death is to realize that death is only a transition and that life is eternal. You do not have to die to release these patterns, nor does anyone close to you. These patterns are released by your awareness and acceptance of your own physical impermanence.

Advanced Energetics

Emerald is the vibrational key for this layer.

Your karmic relationship to children is a feature of the third layer. This includes not only your own children, but also children anywhere in the world. We can only release blockage when we are in a physical body. It is our release valve. Children are old souls in young bodies and deserve all the respect, care and attention they can be given. They have chosen this soul journey once again to allow themselves to release the blockages they carry in their energy bodies and to help others to release theirs. Taking advantage of children, abusing children; physically, emotionally, or psychologically; disrespecting children or knowingly misleading them have created low frequency karmic patterns in the third layer. To release these patterns, we must realize, as parents, that we are only the caretakers and not the owners. If you have no children, this blockage can be released through your close supportive association to children. Golden Topaz is the vibrational key for the third layer.

Karmic patterns dealing with your relationship to your siblings are located in the second layer. Having no brothers or sisters does not mean that there are no low frequency patterns. It means that it will be more difficult for you to get in touch with them and release them. Harboring ill will, resentment, or anger towards your sibling is the reflection of your blockage. To release the blockage from this layer, forgive any perceived injustices or hurts you have experienced at the hand of your sibling. Tell them that you love them and appreciate all the help they have offered, for this is the truth of your relationship. Carnelian is the vibrational kcy for this laycr.

The first layer contains the patterns of your relationship to humanity. This includes people you consider your friends as well as people who are strangers. Karmic patterns here include distrust, disrespect, negative judgment, anger, hate, and fear. Everyone on this planet is worthy of love, respect and support. No one should be judged unworthy of these. It is true that people can do terrible, hurtful things, but these things are done out of ignorance and misperception. These wrongs do need to be addressed, but do not confuse who a person is with what they do. Your inability to separate these two perceptions accounts for the karmic patterns located in the first layer of your Extended Light Body. To release these blockages, view everyone as family. Do not judge them by their failures, but by their strengths. Their failures are a reflection of their blockages, but their strengths are a statement of their perfection. Red Garnet is the vibrational key for the first layer.

As I stated previously, all layers of the Extended Light Body hold patterns involving your relationships and fears. They originated in earlier lifetimes, but their reflection and release is accomplished now. Bach Flower Essences have proven useful in accelerating the release of blockages in this energy level. Crabapple and Olive have a general releasing effect and others accelerate the release of specific blockages. Use your intuition when choosing these essences. When you have released all of these karmic patterns, you will then move into the next level of your energy body called the Earth Body.

Your Earth Body is that part of your energy that extends to the size of the Earth. It contains the karmic patterns you hold from all your lifetimes on Earth in a pre-human form, which include the *Homo habilus* and *Homo erectus* forms. Most patterns here involve issues that negate interconnectedness within the collective, such as murder, enslavement, warfare and the repression of the weak. The perception of separation was not as pronounced then. These pre-human forms were prevalent on Earth for a much longer time than our *Homo sapien* form. You have had many lifetimes in these pre-historic bodies.

The release of karmic patterning in the Earth Body comes with the release of patterns of tribal conditioning. The realization that you belong to the collective called "humanity" and not to isolated clans, groups, countries or religions, allows you to release this low frequency blockage. The clearing at this level is charted in the percentage of released blockage. Vibrational keys to accelerate your release in this level of energy are petrified material from this time era. Having cleared this energy level, you can now move to the next level of your energy called the Solar System Body.

Clearing the Solar System Body involves a different level of existence than what we have worked through so far. This level of energy is as large as our solar system and was a sentient, but not a corporal existence. We had no physical bodies, but took part in a collective mind. There was no death. There were differences, but no separateness within the collective; there was only "we". Separateness appeared to exist, however, in our perception of an external reality. Our karmic patterns at this level resulted from our desire to rule over and manipulate creation. Releasing in this energy layer involves the relinquishing of your desire to control and manipulate others. Vibrational keys to accelerate the release include meteorite fragments, such as Moldavite. Once you have cleared your Solar System Body, you begin to clear your Galactic Body.

    The Galactic Body encompasses the entire Milky Way galaxy and includes karmic patterns you have created in other solar systems than our own in this galaxy. Once again, we existed as mass consciousness. As with the Solar System Body, all karmic debt was incurred by everyone. Most of us have been involved in multiple Solar System existences. The issues of this layer were ones of the perceptions of lack, of not having enough, of insufficiency. This led to patterns of expansion, of hunger, of insatiability and of insignificance. One of 50 billion galaxies in the Universe, our collective chose to expand through diversification and projected itself into a multitude of solar systems and planets. These patterns still reside in the core of our collective unconscious. The release of these patterns is accomplished through the projection of abundance, of sufficiency, of adequacy and of empowerment.

    Finally, We need to clear our karmic patterns in our Universal Body. Your Universal Body is, as you may have guessed, as large as the Universe. The collective mind encompasses all of the galaxies and space in the Universe. The universal collective mind embodies creativity itself. The karmic issues to be released involve assigning fate or destiny, which is the opposite of free will. Assigning order and structure to energy and matter! Releasing these karmic patterns means realizing that the Universe conforms to your perception of it, that God is inherent in every part of the Universe and that it is all alive and conscious. God is one and separation ends!

    Where do we go from there? The desire of

energy is to expand the source; to radiate love. We are becoming as beams of light, radiating love throughout the Universe.

EXPANDED LIGHT BODY

MERCHUR CHART

12	O O O O O O O O O O O
11	12 12 12 12 12 12 12 12 12
10	O O O O O O O O O O O O
9	12 12 12 12 12 10 10 10 8 8 8
8	O O O O O O O O O O O
7	O O O O O O O O O O O
6	12 12 10 10 8 8 8 O O O O O
5	O O O O O O O O O O O
4	O O O O O O O O O O O
3	12 12 12 12 12 12 12 12 12 12
2	12 12 12 12 12 12 12 12 12 12
1	12 12 12 12 12 12 12 12 12 12

Energetic Awakening

This is a sample chart of someone who has partially completed clearing this level of their energy. There are twelve positions representing the depth of the chart. A twelve means that all have cleared; a ten means that all but two have cleared; an eight means that all but four have cleared; a zero means that none in that row have cleared. Some of the layers have completely cleared, as evidenced by having the number 12 at every position in that layer. If a layer resists opening and clearing, special attention must be paid to the karmic issues inherent in that layer. For example, layers 12,8,7,5 and 4 have not yet begun to clear. Layer twelve deals with issues concerning your relationship to your parents. Focus on this relationship and pay attention to what comes up. This procedure should be used for each layer that has not cleared. Check the list at the beginning of the chapter for the respective karmic issues. A completed chart will appear as follows:

Advanced Energetics

EXPANDED LIGHT BODY MERCHUR CHART

12	12 12 12 12 12 12 12 12 12 12 12
11	12 12 12 12 12 12 12 12 12 12 12
10	12 12 12 12 12 12 12 12 12 12 12
9	12 12 12 12 12 12 12 12 12 12 12
8	12 12 12 12 12 12 12 12 12 12 12
7	12 12 12 12 12 12 12 12 12 12 12
6	12 12 12 12 12 12 12 12 12 12 12
5	12 12 12 12 12 12 12 12 12 12 12
4	12 12 12 12 12 12 12 12 12 12 12
3	12 12 12 12 12 12 12 12 12 12 12
2	12 12 12 12 12 12 12 12 12 12 12
1	12 12 12 12 12 12 12 12 12 12 12

Energetic Awakening

Energetic Awakening

Part II

A Soul Journey

Energetic Awakening

Balance and Harmony

There was a time when answers were everywhere, carried on a light breeze, sparkling off a sunlit leaf. They echoed from the joyous calls of birds and were pointed to by shadows on the wall. There was a time that I felt at one with all that is. Now, when I am still, and quiet down my thoughts to a whisper, I wait for answers to again flow into my consciousness. But all that comes is the awareness of stillness. All stories have a beginning and an end, so this can't be a story. I know neither when it began nor if it will end. The only time I know is now.

It was Thursday, I remember because Thursdays Jackie always came to my vegetarian restaurant, "Food For Thought" with her boisterous friends from work. They worked for the city, somewhere in the social services department, and always came on Thursday. Jackie was the loudest of the group. Her musical laughter carried back into the kitchen where I was artfully arranging leaves of lettuce and raw vegetables to compliment the plates of quiche and spinach lasagna I had prepared. It was the noon rush, which meant 60 minutes of craziness, trying to get quality food out to hungry people who only had a half-hour lunch break and had already spent 15 minutes of it looking for a parking place. I was, therefore, somewhat harried as I was told that someone wished to speak with me up front. Jackie stood there with a strange smile on her face, looking at me as though she was confused about something. Jackie always reminded me of a middle age Shirley Temple with her pretty round face and her head full of curls. "Hi. Jackie," I said beaming a smile at her. "Is anything wrong with the food?"

"No," she replied. "The food is delicious as always. I just wanted to tell you that a place has opened up in the course I am offering. I was told that you should take part."

This course she referred to was to be called "Balance and Harmony", and had been recommended to me by my Yoga instructor, Ann. Ann was also taking part. I didn't question who had told her to allow me into the group. I was only happy that I could participate and anxious to get back into the kitchen to continue preparing the food for my customers. At that time, I really didn't know much about Jackie, except that she was held in high esteem by many of my favored customers. I knew that she was somehow involved in "New Age" philosophies and that she ate vegetarian lunches, at least on Thursday. She seemed also to have a pleasant way about her, even when she was loudly and vehemently discussing a topic. Her most impressive feature, however, was her eyes. Her brown eyes would look at you with a soft intensity that did not judge. There was acceptance reflected there. The laugh wrinkles around the eyes revealed humor and a joy of life that also found expression in her full-lipped mouth.

Following the directions she had given me, I finally found her house in a quiet suburb of Portage, Michigan. The house was a reddish color with white trim and had several beautiful pine and oak trees in the large yard. The course began at 7:00 P.M. and there were several cars already there as I arrived. A young woman I recognized vaguely as an infrequent customer in my restaurant opened the door and led me into the dimly lit living room. There was soft guitar music playing somewhere in the background and many candles giving off a warm glow around the room. Comfortable chairs and sofas had been positioned against the walls and were occupied by men and women of various ages. Carol, who had a home massage practice, was there and gave me a quick wave. We had an understanding. Sigi, my wife and I received full body massages several times a month and Carol ate for free in the restaurant. I had a similar arrangement with Ann, who sat quietly chatting with someone I didn't recognize. The others I knew only casually. Everyone seemed to know Jackie, however, as evidenced by the warm hugs and kisses that were exchanged as more people moved into the room. In the end, there were 13 of us, including Jackie, comfortably seated around her large living room.

Jackie was sitting in a large over-stuffed armchair at the far end of the room. She looked different tonight than I was accustomed to. She positively glowed. Her eyes were still pools of richness reflecting the gentle glow of the candles, and a slight smile transformed her face into a vision of serenity.

"We are so happy to see you here tonight," she began in a soft dreamy voice. "Over the course of the next six weeks we want to help you become conscious of the perfection that you all are. We will seek the balance and experience the harmony of ourselves with everything around us, with everything that is. Let us start with a guided meditation."

I was still trying to figure out who the "we" were she was referring to, as some of the participants got into their respective meditative positions, while others sat up straighter and placed both feet squarely on the floor. Being only a novice meditator and never having had much success with it, I felt a little self-conscious. I leaned back into the couch cushion and made myself comfortable, closed my eyes and willed myself to relax. At first, nothing was said. The soft lilting sounds of the guitar music filled the air and blended wonderfully with the aroma smell of Jasmine incense.

"We will take a walk in our minds to a very private place. This is a special place that you will visit often. You are walking down a gently sloping path through a beautiful forest. The trees on either side sway softly in the light breeze and here and there the streaming sunlight breaks through the canopy of leaves creating iridescent patches of sunlight along the way. It is warm and the hum of insects blends with the rustle of trees into a quiet whispering music. You come out of the woods and see a small lake stretched out in front of you. The wind has stopped now and the lake is as clear and smooth as glass. You sit down at the edge of the lake on a comfortable bed of moss and gaze into the still water. You can see the reeds and trees on the opposite shore reflected in the water. You look up and see a songbird flying through an azure blue sky, joyfully singing as it flies. A fish jumps and you watch the ripples move out from the center in perfect circles. The sunlight feels warm against your skin and everything seems to harmonize like a prayer echoing up to heaven. The bird's flight, the jumping fish, the still lake and you are a prayer. A breeze comes up, moving the water in tiny waves. The reeds rustle along the lake as if in answer. The moving air feels wonderfully cool around your body.

Balance and Harmony

The breeze stops and the lake is calm again. Your thoughts are now the lake, quiet and cool and deep. You are the stillness."

I am the stillness? I opened my eyelids slightly and gazed around the room. Everyone was sitting quietly, breathing slowly and regularly. Ann, who sat on the floor in a full lotus position to my immediate right, had a look of rapture on her face. Her index finger and thumb were touching each other to form an "O", while the other fingers extended straight out and her hands were placed at her knees. It was the classical "Buddha" position. It looked uncomfortable, but her face told me that she was unaware of any discomfort at the moment.

Others in the group appeared to be equally as removed, experiencing their special places in their imagination. Jackie, who had lapsed into silence, seemed to be listening with her head cocked slightly to one side. In her hand she was holding something that appeared to be a clear-cut crystal dangling from a golden chain. The crystal was swinging slightly to and fro, occasionally changing its direction of rotation.

Suddenly Jackie spoke again in a soft musical voice. "We will now leave our special places, but will visit them again often. It is evening now on our return. The moonlight illuminates our way as we move along our path to our starting point. The velvety darkness reassures and encourages us. All is in balance; all is in harmony when we reach our path's end. When you are ready, you can open your eyes."

One by one, everyone opened their eyes and stretched as if coming out of a deep sleep. There was a tingling feeling in the room that hadn't been there before. I too felt the warm loving glow that permeated the room. I was wonderfully relaxed and at peace.

Jackie leaned forward and picked up the Bible that lay in front of her, opened it and began to read. "Though I speak with tongues of men and of angels, and have not love, I am become as sounding bronze, or a tinkling cymbal. And though I have the gift of prophecy, and understand all mysteries, and all knowledge; and though I have all faith, so that I could remove mountains, and have no love, I am nothing. And though I bestow all my goods to feed the poor, and though I give my body to be burned, and have not love, it profits me nothing. Love suffers long, and is kind; love envies not; love vaunts not itself, is not puffed up, does not behave itself unseemly, seeks not its own, is not easily provoked, thinks no evil, rejoices not in iniquity, but rejoices in the truth; bears all things, hopes all things, endures all things. Love never fails; but whether there be prophecies, they shall be done away. When I was a child, I spoke as a child, I understood as a child, I thought as a child; but when I became a man, I put away childish things. For now we see in a mirror, darkly; but then face to face; now I know in part, but then shall I know even as also I am known. And now abides faith, hope, love, these three; but the greatest of these is love."

I recognized this beautiful passage as Corinthians I verse 13. Upon finishing, Jackie explained that the path to balance and harmony was a struggle and required a certain discipline and cleansing of the body. We were to drink no alcohol, smoke cigarettes or use any drugs whatsoever for the duration of the six week course. In addition she asked us to reduce or eliminate sex during this period as well. These requests were meant as recommendations to maximize the effects of our lessons. That night, and everyday for the first week, we were to take two tablespoons of pure cold pressed olive oil to purify our internal body. Everyone received small-multicolored ribbons, which were to be worn, pinned to the clothing at all times. Finally we were given small vials of orange blossom oil, which was to be applied to the knee joints, elbow joints and the back of the head twice a day, morning and evening. Everyone took these "suggestion" with a great deal of moaning, groaning, and laughter, but it was clear that there was also a seriousness and a willingness in all present to follow those instruction.

Several members of the group went with Jackie into the kitchen and returned with trays of fruits and vegetables. Jackie proceeded to explain to us that we were working on a particular vibrational level this week. The fruits and vegetables that were passed around were especially chosen because of the particular vibrational frequency they had. Other foods were named, and we were instructed to predominately eat them throughout the week. Many other diet suggestions were given, until finally the meeting broke up and everyone began to leave.

I noticed that occasionally a question was asked, for which she did not have a ready answer. When this happened, Jackie would be silent for a moment and observe the small crystal she held in her hand suspended from the golden chain. After a brief pause, she would answer the question decisively and with authority. Before leaving, I went to her and asked her what she was doing.

"This is a crystal pendulum," she responded smiling. "I use this to put me in contact with my Higher Self when a question is asked that I am not sure about. I use it in much the same way we use a telephone to establish contact to a respected informational source."

I must have looked confused, because she smiled again and continued explaining. "You see," she said, "There is much of reality that we are not aware of. Even death is only a shifting of consciousness from one plane to another. There are many wise souls firmly seated in God consciousness, who are available to instruct us. We rarely are aware of this facet of ourselves, except through our subconscious or in dreams. With a pendulum, once you have learned to use it, you can contact your Higher Self and ask it anything you wish."

" Is our Higher Self the same as the Holy Ghost?" I asked.

" The Holy Ghost is God's messenger, the comforter and carrier of God's word. Your Higher Self is also of God, but unique to you, perfect as you were created. Your Higher Self is in constant contact with the Holy Spirit and with all other Higher Selves. To connect to your Higher Self is to access all knowledge."

This concept was completely new and endlessly intriguing to me. " How does it work?" I wondered aloud, staring at the small, beautifully cut crystal in her hand.

"It's really quite simple," she replied, placing the crystal and chain into my hand. "First of all, you need to establish which direction of rotation means yes and which is no. Just ask." she said, noticing my indecision.

"Which direction means yes?" I asked out loud, feeling somewhat foolish. At first nothing happened, but then there seemed to be a slight movement in the counterclockwise direction. "Which way means no?' I continued feeling encourage by my success. The pendulum continued moving in the same counterclockwise direction. Feeling somewhat ashamed of my performance, I returned the pendulum back to Jackie.

"Don't feel bad, " she said laughing, "it does take some practice and besides, this crystal is attuned to my vibration. You will need to get your own if you want to learn it."

I left feeling elated and with a determination to walk this path as far as it would take me. I could also feel a change occurring within me, fueled by an intense curiosity to know.

Wanting to know the answers had always been a high priority in my life. My studies in science and especially in Biology had not provided me with the answers I sought. They only attempted to categorize and fragment our perception of the world. Although I often found this information fascinating, every question only produced further questions that begged attention. There seemed to be no substance there, only an endless race of questions chasing each other.

My experience with organized Christian religion was even more frustrating. Here I was provided with ready answers to questions that I hadn't even yet formulated in my young head. As I grew older, religion seemed less and less to have anything to do with reality and eventually went the way of Santa Claus and the Easter Bunny. I was left in both cases with a burning curiosity to know and nowhere to take it.

In the late sixties and early seventies, I realized that I was not alone in this search, and that a tremendous number of people were also seeking answers and asking questions. My experimentation with drugs, especially LSD and mescaline, the "mind expanding drugs", opened up new avenues of inquiry for me. Life once again became a mystery and perception a matter of speculation. I was introduced to all manner of religious philosophy and realized that the truths that they all promoted were basically the same, with only shades of variation.

Now, it seemed, I could ask questions and access information from a source that was connected to everything. I wasted no time going to the local jewelry boutique and purchasing a small teardrop-cut glass crystal. I scrounged up an old broken chain I had, and "viola" my pendulum was complete. I immediately began experimenting with it, asking all kinds of questions. The pendulum seemed to be responding, but at the same time, I was also aware that I was moving it. I didn't trust the responses and soon tired of playing around with it. I vowed, however, to continue trying. Jackie believed in it and I believed Jackie.

Karma

The subsequent weeks at Jackie's workshop made a deep impression on me. We began each session with a guided meditation, followed by instruction. Every week we received a new essential oil with a different area of application and a different colored ribbon. A list of foods to eat for the week was presented, along with a special tone pitch to practice during our daily meditations. All of these things were designed to promote the increase of our vibrational frequency.

Vibrational frequency was not an unknown term to me. I had learned that all matter vibrates at different rates. In science, I had been taught about Brownian movement, wavelengths, particle acceleration, etc. What I hadn't considered was that all organisms had a particular vibrational frequency and that it was possible to influence it. The overall effect of the workshop was that we were all raising our vibrational frequencies through the use of oils, sounds, food, color, and meditation.

Jackie told us the story of, "The Hundredth Monkey". "At one time," she said, "all monkeys in the world ate their food as they found it. One day, one monkey washed its food before eating it. It took some time, but slowly other monkeys began copying this procedure, until ninety-nine monkeys were all washing their food before eating it. As the hundredth monkey joined their ranks and washed its food before eating, suddenly in all parts of the earth, wherever monkeys were found, monkeys began spontaneously washing their food. Consciousness," she stated, "expands slowly. There is a point however, where a threshold is reached, let's call it the hundredth monkey, and it suddenly dawns in all minds collectively. There is a level of consciousness, a vibrational level, that if attained by enough people, will impact all of mankind."

    At the fourth session I volunteered to cook spinach lasagna for everyone, which was a favorite dish at my restaurant. I made a list of the things I needed, and everyone kicked in a little money to buy them. I decided to put my pendulum to the test and to use it in the entire decision making process for buying the ingredients. After stuffing the money into my pocket without counting it, I first consulted the pendulum as to which grocery store to use. There were many to choose from, but I was told to shop at Meijers Thrifty Acres. Besides the necessary ingredients, I had also written down some additional things, that I thought would benefit the meal. With every item where a choice was available, I used the pendulum to choose. Sometimes I was told to use the more expensive selection and sometimes the cheapest. Green peppers were four for a dollar, so I took all four. Before going up to the cashier, I again went through every item in the shopping cart with the pendulum. All of those "extras" I had added to the list were deemed unnecessary, so I returned them. Finally, I was informed that everything was fine and that I should proceed to the counter. I had some apprehension my money would not be sufficient, but I decided to follow this through to completion. At the cashier, the food items were tallied up and I counted all the money I had with me. To my disappointment, I didn't have enough. I felt reluctant to take out my pendulum and ask what had gone wrong, because of the people waiting in line behind me. Suddenly, I remembered that I only needed two peppers for the lasagna and had her take the other two off the bill. To my surprise and delight, the sum now exactly equaled the money I had, right down to the last penny! I doubt if the cashier could understand why I was smiling and laughing, but for me this was a wonderful moment, one that was to influence my entire subsequent life. Not only had I discovered that I could use the pendulum reliably, but I had also received "proof", through this double blind test. I discovered that I am guided and can communicate directly to this guidance. Some might contend that this happened purely by chance, but I had stopped believing that life was a long series of random coincidences. To me, this event was concrete and substantial proof, more convincing that anything I could have ever read or been told. I had experienced it!

The subsequent sessions at Jackie's provided me with many opportunities to expand on what I had learned. I was told that love was the guiding force in the universe and that evil was only misdirected purpose. The pendulum helped me to define and process many thoughts and provided me with accurate information on diet, behavior and relationships. Life became mysterious and exciting. I experienced the humor of my guidance and its love and patience. I often felt like a small child talking to a wise old grandfather explaining what was really going on around me.

I acquired a second tool, which helped me to understand situations more thoroughly. My best friend gave me a deck of Tarot cards as a birthday present. I found I was able to give accurate and detailed readings. The advantage to using the cards was that they provided an overall picture of the situation. Most illuminating, however, was the realization that we generally confuse the symptom with the problem. The problem can only be resolved by affecting a change from within. Changing oneself is not easy and is often very painful. Many people prefer to continue blaming others for the problems they have.

    I realize that many of you, who have read to this point, are faced with your preconceptions concerning much of what I have said. My mother, a southern Baptist, was always very concerned about this direction my life had taken. She never tired in quoting scripture to me, which she interpreted to mean that the pendulum, Tarot cards, and meditation, were all instruments of the devil that would most certainly bring me to hell. All I knew was that I felt joyful and at peace. I felt that I was finally in a position to help others who were seeking to find relevant answers to relevant questions.

    At this time Jackie announced that she would offer a follow-up course, which would last eight weeks and be much more intensive than the first. Without exception, everyone who had taken part in the initial course participated in Balance and Harmony 2. "This course," she told us, "will be aimed at raising your vibration levels further and cleansing your energy body of karma. At the culmination of these sessions you will have to choose whether you want to remain on the Karmic Wheel or whether you wish to be free of it."

    Karma is a basic concept of eastern philosophy. It claims that we reincarnate into different lifetimes in our effort to reach nirvana or spiritual perfection. The laws of karma are very similar to the biblical scripture, "an eye for an eye and a tooth for a tooth". It says simply, that you are held accountable for all your transgressions. Karma is the force that draws you to people and situations to resolve issues. Resolution is obtained by applying the principles of love. The Karmic Wheel continues to bring you back after each death for another chance. Removal from the Karmic Wheel would mean that you would no longer be required to return to Earth and that you could proceed to more advanced stages of soul development. You are also no longer guided to people you have previously known. Every day is new and nothing is determined. Karma is a positive force, which allows souls to develop individually. The thought of continuing my spiritual development on a more advanced plane was an appealing concept. Karma binds us to the Earth and always brings us back.

In many ways, the second course was similar to the first. We still had guided meditations and readings from the Bible and other Holy books, but we also started a series of essential oil cleansings. Jackie practiced these cleansings with one or two assistants, until we were all familiar with the procedure. The first cleansing took place with myrrh oil, which was one of the three king's gifts to Jesus. The oil was to cleanse the emotional body of low frequency thought forms.

"Beyond our physical body" explained Jackie, "we have finer and finer layers of energy surrounding us called the aura. The cleansings you receive, will affect four distinct layers; the Astral Body, which is closest to your physical body; the Emotional Body which extends out to about 6 inches from your physical; the Mental Body, extending to 10 inches; and the Spiritual Body, which connects to everything that exists. A newborn baby carries its karmic baggage in the astral layer when it is born. The other layers are generally pure and clean. In the first years, the emotional body develops and emotional blockages can accumulate. Imagine blockage as small puffs of cotton that stick to the aura of the body at certain places. These emotionally generated energy fields vibrate at low frequencies and draw life energy away from the physical body."

"At the age of six," she continued, "the Mental Body begins developing and extends further out from the emotional body. Negative thoughts that the child develops form low vibrational energy fields, which accumulate in the aura. When I say negative, what I am referring to are thoughts and emotions that do not adhere to the principles of love. Emotions such as anger, hate, fear and jealousy, and thoughts of superiority, greed, revenge and lying, shape these fields. Everything we do, think and feel creates something. We are creators and our legacy is what we have created. At the age of twelve or thirteen, the spiritual layer matures. Now you begin to think in abstractions and formulate your concept of God. You can also understand the difference between good and evil and make your choices accordingly. Here also, the wrong choice, or that choice not in harmony with the love principle, can generate a low vibrational field of energy that saps our natural energy and weakens us."

Essential oil cleansings remove the negativity that has accumulated in that particular layer of the aura. Certain oils are effective for specific layers and break up the negative energy fields. The emotional cleansing began by first applying several drops of Myrrh onto the fingers and spreading it over the hands. Beginning at the feet, the hands are held open with the fingers extended. Slowly, the hands are moved upwards along the contours of the body, always remaining several inches from the clothing. As the hands reach the top of the head, the person turns around and the front side of the body is done in the same manner. Emotional negativity is removed through the heart chakra, so the energy is centered on the heart area. When the person giving the cleansing feels that all of the energy has been centered and collected, they proceed to walk away, pulling the low frequency energy with them. They must proceed some distance away before dispelling the collected energy, or it will be pulled back to the person like a rubber band. Generally a distance of 20-30 feet is adequate. The hands are then clapped together several times to dispel the collected energy and it falls apart and dissipates into the surrounding ethers.

 I was skeptical, watching this strange ritual, the first time that a cleansing was performed on me. It was difficult for me to believe that anything was happening and I felt rather silly. The pendulum was used to ascertain whether all negativity had been removed. It sometimes takes several attempts until the body is finally "clean".

 A different cleansing was performed each week and in the interim, we readjusted to our increased energy flow. It was amazing to me how good I began to feel. Patuli oil was used to clean the Astral Body and Frankincense for the Mental Body. Rose oil cleared the Spiritual body of blockage.

 The final cleansings were all performed on the last evening. By this time, we had received cleansings performed on all of the aural layers. Seven of the cleansings cleared specific errors separately from our karmic pasts. They included such things as murder, sodomy, adultery, oppression of others, suicide, sadism and masochism. The last and final cleansing would remove us from the Karmic Wheel. We were asked once again to think about it for a short time and to then decide. My decision had been made long ago. The last cleansing took place with Jojoba oil and we were declared henceforth free of karma. It wasn't until much later that I began to realize the enormity of what I had decided.

Guidance

Vegetarianism was a recent development in our lives. Sigi and I had just finished a five-month bicycle tour of the Yucatan in Mexico and were riding the Pullman up to the California border at Mexicali when we met Ross. Ross was Australian and was watching his 15-speed Peugeot bicycle being unloaded along with ours. He was short and wiry, had a rust brown beard and a slightly hunched over look about him. He was traveling alone and seemed content to accompany us at our moderate pace. As we rode side by side along the Californian coast, he told us about the incredible trip that had brought him to his point. After bicycling completely around Australia, he had taken a boat to Singapore and pedaled up through Southeast Asia to northern Thailand. From there, he flew to Calcutta, India, and continued bicycling through Asia and Europe, finally ending up in England. Working one year in a bread factory in London, Ross then flew to Peru. He bicycled up through South America and Central America to Mexico City. From there he rode the train to Mexicali were we met. Ross was a vegetarian.

We had little money, but were able to supplement our meals by catching fresh fish and finding coconuts along the way. As our money further dwindled, we discovered we could eat very inexpensively and nutritiously by eliminating meats. Ross was instrumental in guiding us through this change of diet. He decided to accompany us back to Michigan when we returned home.

We continued our vegetarian diet in Michigan, more out of necessity than choice. I decided to start a vegetarian restaurant. I reasoned that owning a restaurant would guarantee food on the table. After selling some real estate that had been tied up and borrowing some money from a friend, we began our restaurant and named it "Food for Thought Café". I told myself that we would give it two years. If the business was not showing a profit by then, we would "punish" ourselves by traveling to a South Seas island. It seemed humorous at the time, but made giving up the restaurant two years later almost predetermined.

Ending the course "Balance and Harmony 2" and finishing two years of the restaurant trade occurred at the same time. Our daughter, Zara, had just turned two, so we decided it was time for our promised "punishment". My ability with the pendulum and Tarot seemed to be steadily improving. I was able to intuitively discern the messages they conveyed. Degrees of yes or no answers were apparent in the intensity of the pendulum's swing. The more exact my formulation of the question in my mind, the stronger the pendulum would swing. It was obvious to me that the pendulum was not responding to some outside force, but instead, to subtle movement of my own body. My "Higher Self" was answering the questions through me.

We began the process of selling everything we owned. The restaurant inventory was auctioned off for outstanding debts. After several garage sales and runs to the dump, we reduced everything we owned to two full backpacks. It is difficult to express the tremendous feeling of exhilaration that this freedom gave me. Sigi viewed our forthcoming departure with mixed feelings. She was willing, however, to accompany me with our daughter into the unknown.

We wanted to spend some time visiting my wife's family in Germany. Sigi and Zara flew over first and I followed two weeks later. I flew British Airways through London's Heathrow Airport. After wandering around the crowded terminal, I sat down on an empty bench to wait for my flight. I received information from the pendulum that I should offer a Tarot reading to the next person who set across from me. A minute later an attractive young woman sat down. "Excuse me," I said, not really knowing how to begin the conversation, "but I would like to ask you a rather strange question."

She smiled and said in broken English that she was Italian and that her English was weak. She asked me to speak slowly. I continued, "I would like to offer you a Tarot reading. There will be no charge for it of course."

To my surprise, she seemed genuinely interested. She said that she did have a question that I might be able to help her with. I rubbed several drops of frankincense oil into my temples and asked her to do the same before beginning, to aid in the communication between us. "Lately," she began, "my life has seemed out of control. Everything is chaotic. I want to know why and what I can do about it."

I allowed her to shuffle the cards until they were ready. I have always been intrigued by how the cards are mixed before a reading. The person shuffling invariably stops precisely at the correct instant the cards are ready. I need to cut the cards, occasionally, but generally they are exact. I used the Celtic Cross method, which consists of placing the first two cards face up in the middle of the table. The third card is positioned in a crossing pattern on top of them. The forth, fifth, sixth and seventh cards are placed above, to the left, below and to the right respectively. The eighth, ninth, tenth and eleventh cards are placed in a vertical row to the immediate right, beginning from the bottom. Traditionally, each position and direction has a meaning in the reading. The pendulum allows me to inquire into the detailed meaning of each card.

After checking the direction of each card, I proceeded with the reading. The first two cards provide information that sets the tone of the reading. "You have a relationship with an older man, who you do not love." I explained. "He professes to love you, but he is wealthy and you enjoy the financial security he provides. You are using him and allowing yourself to be used out of motives other than love. This is why your life appears to be out of control."

A second reading gave the details of what she would need to do to rectify the situation. It seemed that she had two alternatives. She could learn to love this man or she would have to leave him. Leaving him would allow her to regain control of her life for now, the cards said, but it would not help her resolve the underlying problem. She must understand that the only basis of a relationship is love. The solution to the problem was for her to change her perception. Shortly afterwards, she caught her connecting flight to Italy.

We planned to stay in Germany for about a month before continuing on to Malaysia. This provided me with ample opportunity to do further research. I had become interested in acupuncture philosophy and techniques some time ago. A friend told me about Claus. Claus had been suffering from a cancerous tumor in his head that had already been removed twice, but continued to grow back. He was now working with a natural healer. I had read about Edgar Cayce's healing abilities and I found it intriguing that he could diagnose and effect a healing without being with the person. I decided to examine this problem from a distance using the pendulum.

    The Hannover Medical Library was located in the suburb of Kleefeld, Germany, just outside the city, near the university campus. It was open to the public and I had no trouble entering. I located a number of books dealing with acupuncture. One German author, Dr. Reinhold Voll, MD, interested me with his books dealing with electroacupuncture. In his 20-years of research and experimentation, he had developed a form of acupuncture using low voltage electrical current, instead of needles, to stimulate the acupuncture points.

    Classical acupuncture uses about 350 points on the body to treat illnesses. The main diagnostic tool is the intuitive analysis of six different pulses taken at the wrists. The pulses are referred to as the shallow, middle and deep pulses. Once the patient is diagnosed, the acupuncturist proceeds to chart a course of treatments that generally include sticking small needles into specific acupuncture points on the body. Sickness arises when blockages or imbalances occur in the body's energy flow. Acupuncture needles, now stainless steel instead of gold or silver as they used to be, are inserted at critical points to remove blockages and balance the body's energy.

    Dr. Voll has expanded the number of points to well over 850 and has established a direct link between individual points and structures within the body. For instance, the point H9 on the heart meridian is located just below the inside corner of the small fingernail. He links it directly to the heart valves, or the aortic valve on the left hand and the pulmonary valve on the right (Leonhardt). His system of diagnosis measures the electrical charge of acupuncture points. The point is only about 1mm in diameter surrounded by a 5mm aureole. The electrical output on the point is higher than the surrounding area and a probe indicates the exact point by emitting a high-pitched noise or flashing a light. Once located, the charge is measured on a scale of 1-100, where fifty is the normal value. Any measurement differing from the norm would indicate a problem in the associated structure.

Using the pendulum, I began to enhance Dr. Voll's charts. I located the points in the interior of the body, where no information is yet available. The points and their corresponding meridians followed the surface of the interior organs. This makes perfect sense to me as a Biologist. It coincides with embryonic development and the specialization of cells.

I used the information and the charts to plot the areas of blockage in Claus. Whenever I located a blockage, I would write down the symptom that would occur with an energy imbalance at this area. The symptoms were very specific, such as the inability to raise the arm above shoulder level. I spent a week in the library researching Clauses' condition, before I felt confident I had found everything that was relevant. The next step was to give Claus a call and meet with him.

When I called him, I introduced myself as a friend of Helga. I explained that I had heard from her about his problem and decided to research it on my own. At first he was perplexed as to why I was taking such an interest in his life, but after a short explanation, he agreed to meet and talk with me.

    Claus was a young man, about 32 years old, medium build and already balding slightly. I was surprised to see no noticeable marks of the disease on his body. He explained that the tumors had been growing under the skull. He also told me that he was now in the care of a doctor that practiced natural healing through visualization. He felt they were making progress in the remission of the tumor. I began showing him the charts and diagrams I had prepared and described the symptoms he should be experiencing. He reported experiencing most of the symptoms during the development of his sickness. Although he was very pleasant and impressed with the amount of preparation I had done, he intended to continue his present treatments with his doctor. I gave him the information I had and we parted. I felt as though the work had been well worth the effort.

    I went back to the medical library. This time, however, I was interested in learning something completely unknown. I began by scanning down the list of subject areas with the pendulum. From there I would proceed to the designated books dealing with this subject matter. I would then remove that particular book indicated and open it to the table of contents. Eventually, my search would lead me to the exact page, paragraph, sentence or word that I was directed to and I would write it down. After hours of research, I sat down and used the pendulum try to make some sense of it all. The phrases and words I had written, seemed disconnected and random. Some dealt with specific symptoms a sick person would feel, such as fever and chills and trembling, while others were associated with different areas of the world. There were also sentences dealing with dentistry and the mouth.

With the help of the pendulum, I began to access information that I had never read or heard of before. The Earth, according to this information, also possessed energy flow lines or meridians and acupuncture points spread across its surface and continuing into the interior. The meridians seemed to mirror the meridians of the human body. Those that ran along the internal organs in my diagrams coincided with those under the crust of the Earth. The information I accessed described the palate of the Earth, which was located in the region of Portugal and Spain. The coal from that region was analogous to our teeth. Mining in that area was affecting the Earth in much the same way a person might suffer with a toothache. It caused shifts in climatic zones and trembles in the form of earthquakes. The idea seemed so absurd it was almost believable.

I began to develop this idea further by purchasing a large wall map of the world and charting the meridian flow lines of the Earth. We have been taught that the Earth formed from a collection of cooled and condensed matter that ultimately became the spherical body with which we are now familiar. Precious metals and mineral deposits are distributed in random deposits around the Earth. I was convinced that there was no such thing as randomness in the universe. The problem was in recognizing the inherent patterns. I hypothesized that the key to locating precious deposits in the Earth was to identify the electromagnetic flow lines. I reasoned that by locating the meridians, I could then match up known deposits around the globe and a recognizable pattern would lead me to the Earth's treasures.

Using a pendulum as a divining tool, I began

to chart the energy pathways on the world map. I marked a point on the map when the rotation of the pendulum reversed itself. I would then check the direction of energy flow and make another point. This process continued until the meridian came to an end. Quite often this end position was preceded by a spiral or vortex, which rotated either clockwise or counter-clockwise.

      I was astonished to see the structures that became apparent. They looked like textbook illustrations of our own internal organs (see map 1 at the end of the book). I saw the digestive tract, beginning with a double line at the mouth in Portugal and widening into the palate in northern Spain. It narrowed again at the border of Spain and France and proceeded up the Atlantic coastline of France, looking like the esophagus. In Germany, it widened again. While one line continued along the northern coast of Germany and Poland, the other line dropped down to include Switzerland and northern Italy. It traced a path through Slovakia and into the Ukraine, doubling back again to parallel the adjacent line at Lithuania (stomach). They continued close together and parallel, north of Moscow, and then began a series of convolutions and turns through what was formerly known as the western Soviet Union (small intestine). They ran into Mongolia and China, looking like a picture of the large intestine. Finally, the lines converged in northern Afghanistan (the anus). As ludicrous as this may sound, the concept fits the idea of viewing the Earth as a living organism.

      Southeast Asia and India mirrored the sex organs, with the Earth having both male and female sexes. The penis extended down from China to Cambodia and the vagina with clitoris included Thailand,

Malaysia and part of Indonesia. The testicles and ovaries were located in India and Pakistan and the uterus was in Tibet. A readily identifiable liver covered most of Iran, Saudi Arabia and Turkey, with the bile duct and gallbladder extending into Greece, and Italy. The bladder covered a large portion of northern Africa, extending as far west as Algeria and south to Zaire. There were large gland-like structures in western and southern Africa. A lung took up most of the western half of South America. The Amazon basin has often been referred to as the green lung of the world. The heart of the world was perfectly outlined in the western United States, extending from its apex near Los Angeles, into the Rocky Mountains, New Mexico and Arizona. The different hemispheres and lobes of the brain were identifiable in Pacific Ocean, with the hypothalamus and pituitary gland including the Polynesian islands. There were other structures of lines spiraling into themselves. These structures apparently represented sensory apparatus, like the eyes, ears, etc. Some shapes looked exactly like the endocrine glands of the body and coincided with the tremendous diamond finds in southern and eastern Africa, Venezuela, and southern Brazil.

    Several other phenomena also became apparent during this period, such as my heightened physical sensibility around people who were ill. This was most obvious around my German mother-in-law. A pacemaker regulated her heart and her thyroid gland had long been dysfunctional. Whenever I was in her immediate vicinity, I experienced extreme discomfort in these areas of my own body. It was a physical pain that I could only explain on a vibrational level. Bodies vibrate at different frequencies, depending on age, the extent of blockage and their state of health.

The vibration of a child is higher than that of an adult and the vibrational frequency of a sick person is lower than that of someone healthy. There is a resonance that occurs between energy fields. I had reached a point were I could discern between my own energy field and that of others.

A second remarkable change I experienced was initiated by my decision to be celibate. I wanted to channel all of my vital energy into my spiritual development. This was a momentous decision for me! As a Taurus, sexuality had always commanded a dominant position in my life. Sex was a basic need. Suddenly, it was being sacrificed for the development of the soul. My wife accepted this pronouncement with some reservations, but she went along with it. What choice did she have? All sexual thoughts and urges disappeared after two weeks! It was as if my conscious choice to be celibate had triggered an off switch in my brain.

We had left the United States poorly funded for the journey we planned. I sold a piece of jewelry my mother had given me as an heirloom for a modest price and went to the bank to check my old accounts. There was none left. The teller, however, located seven hundred German marks in an old interest bearing account I had forgotten. We purchased three one-way tickets to Kuala Lumpur, Malaysia the next week. Spirit was clearly making the way free for us.

Asia

Kuala Lumpur was a bustling, modern city. The standard of living was surprisingly high, as were the prices. It was clear that we could not spend much time in Malaysia given our economic circumstances. We boarded a train headed for Thailand. The warm weather was definitely a plus. Fresh exotic fruits were abundantly displayed in all market places. It was winter in Germany when we left, but here, our heavy winter clothes were shed for good.

The scenery on either side of the train was jungle interspersed with small villages. The cars were full, but not crowded, as we journeyed through northern Malaysia and into southern Thailand. I had been to Thailand on a previous trip to Southeast Asia and I had loved it. I was single then, traveling with friends. The exotic climate together with the kindness of the people appealed to me in a way that few other countries had. Buddhism, the predominant religion, creates an atmosphere of peacefulness and respect. The train slowly wound its way up the narrow tract of southern Thailand.

We had been told about several beautiful resort islands off the coast and set our sights on the island of Ko Samui in the Gulf of Thailand. Not only was the island accessible by ferry, but it was also reported to be simple and inexpensive; the perfect place for an extended stay. After a four-hour boat trip and a lengthy taxi ride, we finally found a small resort overlooking the Gulf. It was idyllic and cost about $4 U.S. a night to stay. We ate our meals in a thatched, open-air restaurant on the beach. The most expensive dish cost one dollar.

It was a wonderfully relaxing time for us. I continued my reading about electroacupuncture, gave Tarot readings to other tourists and explored the energy points of the area. The first Earth acupuncture point I found was in the resort compound and looked like every other piece of ground surrounding it. I used the pendulum to locate its exact position and determined its size to be about 12 inches in diameter. I wasn't certain how to use the point, so I got a chair and placed it next to the point with my feet directly in the center. I meditated for thirty minutes on the spot and remember feeling nothing out of the ordinary. It wasn't until the next morning that I realized that something was terribly wrong. My entire body hurt! Every fiber of my body, from the tips of my toes, to my fingertips, was in pain. There was no other explanation for my condition other than my use of the Earth point. Guidance told me that I had overdone it and that five minutes would have been more than adequate. The point needed to be used sparingly until I built up a tolerance for the Earth energy. The discomfort slowly receded from my extremities until it was concentrated in the area around my navel. It took nearly two weeks until the pain completely disappeared. My lesson had been uncomfortable, but it provided the best evidence I could have been given as to the validity of this energy. I had experienced it!

I began looking around the island and was guided to several more Earth acupuncture points. One point in particular was interesting, because of its intensity. We experienced this point's vibration two hundred yards away from where it was located in a large Buddhist compound. Someone had capped it to its exact size with cement and etched a symbol into the cap. Others were evidently also aware of these energy "springs". I began using the energy of the points to work on increasing my own vibrational frequency. I wasn't sure what effect they would have on me, but I hypothesized that a higher vibration might lead to improved health.

After two months on Ko Samui, our funds had dwindled to about $500. We called an acupuncturist friend in Japan, but he informed me that Japan was very expensive and he couldn't pay an apprentice. Our next choice was to fly to Katmandu, Nepal, where living costs were markedly lower.

I had been to Katmandu before and loved the experiences it had provided. "The City of 1001 Gods", as it is called, is located in the Katmandu Valley in the Himalayas. Its exotic charm prevails over the stench of its open sewers and unwashed bodies. We took up residence in a recently built four-story hotel that catered to tourists. The accommodations were primitive and inexpensive, which suited us well.

I continued to monitor my vibrational frequency after using the Earth acupuncture points in Thailand. What if the Earth also possesses a chakra system? Could I locate an Earth chakra and increase my vibrational frequency even higher? There was no doubt in my mind that Katmandu contained such a point. The city fairly oozed with energy! It didn't take long to locate the chakra in the center of the city. It was as if everyone around was already aware of it. The point was located in a large circular courtyard surrounded by buildings. It was covered by literally hundreds of small shrines and altars. Pilgrims would move around it in a counterclockwise direction, prostrating themselves on the ground as they offered their prayers and supplications. The chakra was much larger than an Earth acupuncture point, extending to approximately 20 feet in diameter. I could not understand why more people were not consciously picking up on this energy. They seemed to know of these points on an unconscious level, but there was no awareness. Awareness appeared to be the key to tapping this boundless energy!

A European Buddhist enclave was also visiting Katmandu at this time. They were attending a series of lectures given by a Tibetan monk. The lectures included information on Tibetan Buddhism and their system of beliefs. I was interested in these lectures for another reason. I wanted to understand why Jesus Christ was the initiator of Christianity, instead of becoming a Buddhist himself. Several books claimed to have traced the movements of Jesus during his "lost years", or between the age of 12 and 34 years old. The Bible gives no accounting of this time, but assumes he worked as a carpenter until he appeared on that dusty road to gather his disciples. The authors claim to have read documents that traced the movements of Christ into India and Nepal. If this were true, he would have been familiar with Buddhist doctrine. Even if these reports were not true, I am sure that Buddhists were represented in Judea as well. What did Christ understand that Buddhists and Jews did not?

My mother had given me a Christian Bible, King James Version, before we left America to begin our trip. Traveling affords ample opportunities to read and I had read the New Testament during our stay in Thailand. Having left the Baptist Church when I was fifteen, I was more than a little skeptical about religious dogma. Given so many intelligent people that adhere to Christianity, I felt it deserved another chance.

Jesus told us that Heaven was within, which paralleled my own ideas. He also said that what he had attained, so would others after him. I was determined that I would be one of those others. The truth contained in the rendition of Christ's life on Earth was undeniable for me. I accepted Christ into my heart. The rest of the dogma associated with Christianity, I was less sure about.

I attended several of the initial lectures in an old Buddhist temple in the city. The monk spoke Tibetan, which was then translated into German and English. Since I understood both languages, I was privileged to hear them twice. I consulted with my pendulum, as I listened, to try to discern myth from reality. The main strengths of the Buddhist beliefs were its love and respect for all life and its firm commitment to spiritual growth. These were the same strengths I recognized in early Christian faith. An image came to my mind's eye that seemed to clarify the situation for me. I saw a Buddhist and a Christian standing back-to-back, facing in opposite directions. The Buddhist was looking back over the eons of evolutionary and spiritual development into the Void. The Christian was looking ahead, into the fullness and into the light. It was only a matter of perspective. Once I realized that, I no longer attended the lectures. My question had been answered.

A European couple staying at the same hotel asked me why I was not at the lectures anymore, so I told them what I had understood. Ulli, a young man from Denmark, disagreed with my synopsis and argued with me. His German girlfriend, Ulrike, supported his viewpoints, so I suggested that we do a Tarot reading for clarification. They both agreed and I asked

Spirit to show us a reading that would leave no more room for question. It was a different reading than I had done before, with a swing or key card as the crossing card. The swing card was the King of Cups, which represented Christ in this reading. The reading was so powerful and clear, that there were no more questions asked afterwards. They went back to their rooms to think about what they had learned. The next day they both asked me how they could become Christians. I told them to recite the "Lord's Prayer" and invite Christ into their hearts, which they did.

After the lectures, Ulrike had to return to Germany, but Ulli decided to accompany us. By this time, our funds were almost exhausted. Guidance indicated that I still needed to do something before leaving Katmandu. I received a small diamond from my stepmother that she had won in a raffle, before leaving America. I wasn't sure what to do with it, so I had taken it along. I was told that I needed to have it surgically implanted in my palm at the H8 acupuncture point in my left hand. This point was on the heart meridian and was to be used to focus heart energy when doing hands-on healing. This request, however odd, seemed in line with my spiritual growth. I began to look for a doctor that would be willing to perform the surgery.

My two-year-old daughter, Zara, became my guide on this quest. Carrying her in my arms, we began our quest in Katmandu to find the right doctor. At every street corner I would ask Zara the way to go and she would point left, right, or straight ahead. Finally, she pointed to a door with a sign indicating it was a doctor's office. It was padlocked shut for the day and when I examined the lock more closely, I was amazed to see a small diamond etched into the metal by the manufacturer. It was a Diamond lock. It was evident to me that she had led me to the correct address. The next day, I went to the office and explained to the doctor that I was conducting an experiment. I said I believed that the stone, when placed under my skin, would increase my ability to heal people. He seemed skeptical, but agreed to perform the operation for fifty American dollars. The diamond was implanted that afternoon. The surgery went well, except in its final phase. After disinfecting the incision, the doctor seemed to forget to disinfect the stone before he sewed it into my hand. I noticed this, but trusting that everything was in perfect order, I didn't mention it. I went back to the hotel and we made plans to travel to India.

Lessons

One of the most inexpensive places to be in Asia is India. We made our way down from Katmandu into India with small busses and then trains. Riding on the top of the bus with the luggage allowed us to enjoy a wonderful view and best of all, the fresh air. Ulli helped to take care of Zara and was a superb companion.

In Thailand, I received the information that we should adopt a young boy from Nepal. I even went to the Nepalese adoption agency to inquire about the process of adoption. I was told that it was possible, but only until the child became eighteen. At that point he had to return to Nepal to serve in the military. I asked Zara if she would like to have a big "Bruder", which was the German word for brother. Zara said she would welcome a big "Buddha". Ulli seemed to be that big brother that Zara hoped for.

I sold my Pentax camera to give us some more expense money and checked our luggage to see if anything else was expendable. Every time we moved from one place to another, I used the pendulum on every item we still carried with us. I left those things the pendulum indicated. Our packs became lighter and lighter as we continued. If our shoes or clothes became worn, we always seemed to find someone with exactly the item we needed. Eventually, our path brought us to Jaipur in the province of Rajasthan, about 200 kilometers south of New Delhi. The city of Jaipur is enclosed by a high pink wall and is known appropriately as "The Pink City". We took a room at "The Evergreen Hotel" outside of the city, which we later dubbed as "The Never-green Hotel". Rajasthan is arid with an extremely low humidity and almost no precipitation.

Our mail had been forwarded to Agra, in northern India, so I made plans to journey there. Sigi was to remain at the hotel and wait for our return. I expected money to be sent, which we now sorely needed. I had sent an encrypted message to Jackie, explaining our need and I felt sure she would respond. I knew that, whatever happened, we were being cared for and protected by Spirit.

Our journey to Agra was uneventful, but Ulli and I somehow got split up when we reached the city. The mail contained some letters, but no money, so I took Zara to the Taj. The Taj Mahal is the most famous edifice in Agra. Begun by an Indian king as a monument to his beautiful wife, it was finished by his son, who took the wife and put his father in prison. The king was interned opposite the Taj and forced to watch the completion of the building. I was confident I would see Ulli there. We stayed until they closed at 10 P.M., admiring the buildings and the gardens. Visitors were ushered out of the grounds through two doors. We left through the narrow one. (Luke 13:24)

I was becoming increasingly aware of the symbolism and synchronicity in our life. The world was revealing aspects of itself that had always remained hidden before. I was not that certain of the world my senses presented me anyway. The Buddhist concept of "Maya", or the world of sensory illusion was an idea I could relate to. Reading the books of Carlos Castenada about his many year apprenticeship with the Yaki Indian sorcerer Juan Matus, lead me to believe that there is much more to reality than meets the eye. I began to try to discover this unknown world of the spirit. The pendulum aided me greatly in my quest. It provided insight and explanations that I could not gain elsewhere. I viewed my extensive use of the pendulum like a course at the university: Mystery 101. I followed the directions of the guidance I received through the pendulum the same way I would listen to a wise professor. I did hope, however, for more direct guidance. It was wearisome formulating questions for the yes or no answers and my conclusions were always subject to error. I desired a "purer" form of communication. It was at this point that my pendulum left me.

I had used many pendulums to this point. My first one was a teardrop-cut crystal on a short gold chain. The size of the crystal increased, as I was able to channel more and more energy. I was asking a question in our hotel room in Agra, when the pendulum circled so fast, that the centrifugal force pulled it from my fingers. It rolled across the room and fell down a hole filled with water. It was completely obvious to me that my guidance was no longer to be conveyed through the pendulum. Instead, my daughter became my guide.

Everyone thinks his or her children are special, but Zara had always seemed like a very old soul. Even her baby pictures mirrored a demeanor that looked almost alien. Jackie told us in a reading that Zara had indeed lived much longer than either of us. Suddenly, our rolls were reversed. Now she became my teacher! I was the child and she was the wise being explaining to me the way the world really worked. The lessons began that night in Agra.

It was dark after we left the Taj and we went

to a small open-air restaurant for something to eat. A generator, running loudly in the background, provided electricity for the lights. During our meal, Zara suddenly smiled and said, "Lights out". Seconds later, the generator stopped and plunged the entire area into darkness. While I was still wondering how she could have known, she said "Lights on", and the lights came back on. I asked her how she knew that, but she only smiled mysteriously and continued eating as though nothing had happened. This trick happened several more times during the next days.

  We took a bicycle-rickshaw ride outside of the city after dinner and enjoyed being pulled around by the driver. The night was warm and neither of us was sleepy. We heard singing in the distance and decided to investigate. The driver brought us to a church, where Easter Mass was being held. The church was already packed as we took seats in a forward pew. It was a beautiful ceremony, full of singing and tradition. The donation basket was passed around and I pulled some money out of my pocket to contribute. Change fell on the floor, but Zara told me to leave it "for the cleaning lady". The night was rich with symbolism and synchronicity. Everything we were involved in suggested an underlying pattern or purpose.

  We began our trip back to Jaipur the next day. Ulli was still nowhere to be found and I assumed he had given up and headed back. Unexpectedly, a small orange sliver of glass stuck into Zara's hand. "Ouch" she said and proceeded to pull it out and stick it into her mouth. I told her to spit it out, but she swallowed it instead and told me not to worry. Trusting Spirit, I accepted it. There was nothing I could do about it anyway.

  We rode the bus through the dry, uneven landscape. Pointing out the window, Zara proceeded to insist that we get out of the bus now. She said we had to go to church and gestured towards a hill in the distance with a large radio tower on top of it. I tried to explain to her that it would not be possible to leave the bus here, but she continued to insist and became very agitated. I went to the front of the bus and explained to the driver that my daughter needed to go to the bathroom immediately. The driver was reluctant to stop until I described how unpleasant her bowel movement would be on a crowded bus. He halted the bus and allowed us to climb out. Once outside, I told him to drive on without us. At first he refused to leave, but it soon became apparent that we weren't getting back in. Finally, he drove on, leaving us at the side of the road.

  I picked Zara up and began walking towards the distant hillside. I wasn't sure why I was following these directions, but it seemed as though an unspoken warning was telling me that I must comply. The sliver of glass that Zara had swallowed was still in her digestive tract and I felt that a lack of faith on my part could have dangerous consequences. Carrying Zara on my shoulders, we walked along a dry riverbed. A large black cobra suddenly slithered along side of us about six feet away. I saw it as the symbol of Satan and yelled, "Get ye behind me Satan". Zara told me not to be so loud, because I was scaring it. Shortly afterwards, the snake disappeared down a hole in the ground.

  People began to emerge from near-by dwellings and flock towards us from all directions. Two men actually carried a bed out of a house for us to relax on and offered us food and water. A young man presented himself as the English teacher of the area and inquired politely what we were doing here. Instead of answering him, I asked him if he would mind translating to the others. By then, our entourage had expanded to about fifty men, women and children. He agreed and I began to speak. "Children are our gift from God to teach us how to see the truth. They see reality as it is, unclouded by biases, prejudices and faulty belief systems. Honor and love your children, but most of all listen to what they say. God speaks through their mouths."

    Looking at their faces as the teacher translated, I saw they were amused by my utterances. This tall white stranger appearing out of nowhere into their midst, telling them about God's truth. As I continued talking, the whole scene became almost festive. The teacher said he would escort us back to the highway and flag down the next bus for us. He told me that there were people in the city that could help me. I laughed and asked him if he thought I was crazy. He nodded affirmative. "Well, I think you are all crazy" I said as we boarded the bus. We waved good-bye and were on our way once more.

    Zara began teaching me how to see the brightness of people's aura. "Good people are bright," she maintained, "and bad people are dark." It also seemed that the possessions of good people were also bright. I was still trying to understand what she had told me when the bus stopped for the evening.

    It was dark by now and the area was filled with busses and crowds of people. The driver indicated that this was the final destination for his bus and that we would have to transfer to another. I held Zara in my arms as I attempted to orient myself in this sea of humanity, until I heard Zara say with a laugh. "Now let's have some fun." At that point she began crying and screaming at the top of her lungs. I had no idea what was going on or what I should do in the darkness. It seemed like a test she was putting me through to make use of the information she had previously conveyed to me. I scanned the crowd, which by now had all turned toward us to see what the child was screaming about. A man detached himself from the surrounding bodies and asked me if he could be of any help. He was wearing a clean white outfit that seemed bright in the reflected light. I explained to him that we needed a bus to Jaipur, but had no idea where to find it. He told me to give him our money and he would buy us our tickets. I pressed our Rupees into his hand and he disappeared into the crowd. "Oh well" I thought, "there goes our money."

  A few minutes later, he reappeared with two tickets and some change and escorted us over to the correct bus. It seemed I had passed my test, because Zara stopped crying and was her normal cheerful self again. We boarded the bus, which already had several passengers. Two people in particular drew our attention, a young mother and her child. The mother was trying to quiet her child, who was crying and fussing. I began talking to the child in English as I would an adult. I told it that its mother didn't know any better and that it had to have patience with her. Zara looked at the child's tearful eyes and told me, "She doesn't understand yet. Wait!" she said and the lights all went out. They went back on several seconds later and she said, "Now speak." I began talking to the child again. As I watched, a look of amazement and then comprehension crossed its face. Then it really screamed! "It can understand you now" said Zara with a slight smile.

  We arrived back in Jaipur and returned to the

hotel. Ulli had returned a day earlier and Sigi was sick with worry. She made it clear that she would never allow me to take Zara anywhere again without her. We now had to decide what we were going to do with almost no money and no return tickets home in the middle of India. I was sure Spirit would help us. Once we were settled back into the room, Zara told me she needed to go to the toilet. I took her and stood by as she proceeded to expel an exorbitant amount of feces. With the last push she assured me that the glass was no longer in her system. I took her word for it.

Onslaught

I started my fast before we left Nepal. My goal was for thirty-four days, a day for each year of my life. The Bible tells about the prophets fasting for forty days before receiving their visions. I had fasted occasionally in the past, generally 3 to five days, but this fast would be the most extensive one. There are many methods of fasting, depending on what you want to accomplish. Already very thin, I was not interested in losing weight, but instead, saw it as an opportunity to detoxify the body. My main emphasis this time, however, was to weaken the physical, which I assumed would strengthen the spiritual. I also expected an extended fast to lift the veil of illusion to help me to perceive correctly.

The fast consisted of water, and occasionally a little honey, to keep my blood sugar from crashing. The first two days are always the most difficult. The body tells you it needs food in no uncertain terms as your blood sugar levels plummet. By the third day, your liver kicks in and begins metabolizing your glucose reserves. Your fat reserves are then broken down and burned for energy, and finally, in extreme cases, your muscle tissue and other body cells are sacrificed for fuel. I have read several well-documented reports of a woman named Therese Neumann, who purportedly ate and drank nothing for thirty-five years with no loss of weight or body fluids. (Talbot) Her nourishment and energy was obtained entirely metaphysically. After two weeks of fasting I was still feeling great. I no longer had any sense of hunger and was able to perform normal daily functions. I had become considerably thinner, but it did not affect my disposition. By the time I returned from Agra, I was entering my third week of fasting.

My study of the Bible had intensified. I was especially interested in the Book of Revelations. I saw the narrative of John the Divine as non-chronological events that spanned eons of time. Analogous to dreaming, they seemed to jump from the present, to the future, to the distant past, in their accounting. Meanings became clear that I had never considered before, for instance the passage in Revelations 2:17. "He that hath an ear, let him hear what the Spirit says unto the churches: To him that overcomes, will I give to eat of the hidden manna and will give him a white stone, and in the stone a new name written, that no man knows except he that receives it."

The white stone was the white quartz crystal I used in my pendulum and the hidden manna was the hidden energies that could be tapped. The "new name" was my soul name, the name of my Higher Self. Other Bible passages took on a whole new connotation when examined more carefully.

I was praying and meditating frequently during the day and was given the information that I was ready for Christ to merge his energy with my own. The merging of energies would allow me to develop my abilities to a much greater extent. The time was set and I waited with excitement and some apprehension. I didn't know what would happen. Would that part of me I know as myself disappear and be assimilated like some Star Trek version of the Borg, or would we both be in the same body? I made up my mind that it didn't matter what happened to me. The important thing was that Christ's energy would become a part of who I am. I waited in suspense as the moment approached and when it arrived, it was as gentle as the touch of a feather.

    I became strong in spirit, but weak in body as my fast continued through the forth week. My body was very thin now, having lost a great deal of muscle tissue. I managed a short walk every day, but was soon exhausted and returned to bed. Sigi did the chores and played with Zara, while I mostly slept. I broke the fast on day thirty. Guidance told me I had reached the point I needed to attain and that I could resume eating. I had begun to constantly entertain thoughts of food and eagerly planned for my first delicious meal. When it came to eating it, however, I was disappointed. The food had tasted so much better in my fantasy than in real life. In any case, my stomach had shrunken to the point where only a small quantity of food already filled me up.

    I felt much stronger after a few days of eating regularly. My hand had almost healed from the infection that had developed from my operation. It was then that I began receiving information from all around me. Every peacock's call, every breeze or reflection of the sunlight off of a leaf told me something. They didn't actually talk to me, but instead seemed to echo my thoughts. Nature was giving me instant confirmation on my thoughts. I only needed to formulate a question in my mind and wherever I looked, I saw the answer. A young Swiss man had severe digestive problems and looking into the clouds, I could clearly see cloud movement resembling an amoeba. I diagnosed him as having amoebic dysentery.

    A young girl we met from an adjacent room complained of terrible pains in her abdomen. Looking at the wall in the room, I saw what I interpreted as a picture of the uterus and the two ovaries. I told her she had an infection in her ovaries and asked her whether I should attempt to heal her. When she assented, I passed my left hand slightly above her body over the affected area. A short time later, she fell to the floor and had to be taken to the hospital by an ambulance. When she returned, I asked her friend what had happened. He replied that the tubes connecting the kidneys to the bladder had both collapsed. The doctors had given her a muscle relaxant, which allowed the tubes to open up again. Something was terribly wrong! Instead of healing her, I had somehow forced the infection to her kidneys. I decided not to try healing anyone else until I discovered what was happening.

    It was then that the assault began. I felt that something was amiss when the information I was receiving started to turn ominous. People appeared strange and distorted to me, as though they were misshapen or deformed. Only Sigi, Zara and a Christian doctor we had met looked normal. Everyone else looked like they were wearing a lifetime of sins on the outside of their bodies. Out of their eyes came looks of greed, vice and hate. I began receiving information that my wife and child would be injured if I did not do what I was told. I thought an aural cleansing for the emotional body would help my situation and asked Sigi to perform it. Using myrrh oil, she swept her hands through my emotional body and centered them over my heart chakra to remove the blockages. The next thing I knew, something knocked her across the room and onto the floor. I watched in horror as the light in her eyes faded, before she recovered. Both of us were very frightened now and tried to figure out what to do. I put strings of garnets around our necks for protection, but Sigi insisted that we go down to a small catholic church we had noticed on the edge of town. We hailed a rickshaw and went down to the church.

When we arrived at the church, an old priest met us and invited us in. I tried to explain that we were under attack by some demonic being and that we didn't know how to fight back. He heard me out before he said, " I am an old man. I have had the typhoid fever twice and only three-fourths of my heart still works. I don't know why God still keeps me around. But I have learned one thing. There is no greater power in Heaven or on Earth than Jesus Christ! Forget your gemstones or whatever else you have and put your trust in Christ." He told me to raise my head like a young Christian gentleman, and walk out of that church with no fear in my heart. "You will be protected," he said.

His words allowed us to steady ourselves and walk out of the church to face the continued onslaught. Heading back to the hotel in the rickshaw, I received a steady stream of information saying that around the next corner a bus would come and smash into us. I even knew the license number of the bus. Sure enough, a bus careened around the corner with that exact number and drove straight for us. At the last moment, it veered away, just missing our rickshaw. All I could do was remember the priest's words and ask God for our protection. Somehow, we managed to return safely to our hotel.

The demon, as I now referred to it, began to assail me physically. I felt a great force around my navel area trying to push into my body. By force of will, I held it in check as we struggled. Walking outside, I was surrounded by an intense wind that threw sticks and small stones on all sides of me. I received the information that I should cut my hand off, because it was tainted. The wind blew open the Bible to Matthew 5:30. "And if thy right hand offend thee, cut it off, and cast it from thee; for it is profitable for thee that one of thy members should perish, and not that thy whole body should be cast into hell." Fortunately for me, the hand in question was my left.

I told Sigi what I was getting and she told me I was crazy. She said that loving God would never require us to sacrifice our hand to appease it. I had to admit she made a good point, but I couldn't turn the information off. I no longer trusted my own decisions as being rational and told her I would use her grasp of reality as my sounding board in making any future decision. Every time I received information from that point on, I ignored it. When something beckoned, I turned away. It was hard, but after three days of battle, it stopped. The information stopped, the attacks halted and it was calm again. Now we had to figure out how we could get out of this jam.

By this time, our money was completely gone. The Swiss man, who I had diagnosed with dysentery, and his girlfriend loaned us fifty dollars to get to New Delhi and we gave him our gold wedding rings as collateral. We went to the American Consulate and said we were destitute and wanted to return back to the United States. The officer asked us if we had any family that could wire us some money and let us make some phone calls. My mother said she would see what she could manage and before long we had enough money for return trip tickets home. We met the Swiss couple later that day in town and retrieved our rings.

Recovery

We returned to the United States and began picking up the pieces of our lives. Our first reaction was to attribute the whole episode to temporary insanity and get on with life. I refused to have anything more to do with the pendulum or Tarot cards. I envisioned a more normal existence where life was a product of the senses and not guided by unseen forces. I paid a visit to Jackie to see what her perception of our experience was.

Jackie was fascinated by our accounts and congratulated us on our ability to have survived our ordeal. "You went through a very difficult test," she concluded after hearing our story. "You thought the path to enlightenment was one of power. Power begets power. The more powerful you became, the more you attracted powerful beings to you. Power is a by-product of the path, but not its goal. The path to enlightenment is by way of the heart!"

She continued as I was pondering her words. " The mind is a wonderful tool, but it is also the extension of the ego and can get you into all kinds of trouble. Evil is what you find on the path with no heart. When you saw everyone as distorted and misshapen, you were seeing the world as the entity you battled saw it. Through this perception, the world and those in it appear hideous and repulsive. Can you imagine what it must be like to be in this frame of mind for all eternity? We must have compassion for these suffering beings. To never experience God's love and see His light is truly to be in hell." She paused to let her words sink in.

"As I said before; you were tested. The lesson was to experience the path of power and mind and to turn from both. You could have stayed in that space forever had you not." Jackie twirled her pendulum reflectively before she resumed speaking. "You have learned the road not to follow and have gained important knowledge and tools. Now you must travel the road that your heart will lead you. It will take you the distance and lead you to the light."

Before we left, Jackie told me that I still had an Entity attached to my energy body and offered to help me get rid of it. She claimed that it was a particularly low frequency being that told her it didn't believe in God. She performed a cleansing where she sliced its energy body into small pieces and sent them into the Earth. She also gave me the name of a doctor friend of hers that would get rid of the diamond still embedded in my left hand.

I visited the doctor the next week and he agreed to remove the stone in exchange for some sapphires I had brought back from India with me. The surgery went well, except that he had difficulty finding the stone at first. He did tell me that I had been very lucky the infection had not reached my blood stream or I would have had severe blood poisoning.

We moved back to Germany several years later, after our second daughter was born. Our lives had become more or less normal, whatever that means. I began using the pendulum again sparingly. Where before, I had followed its directions without question, now I always ran the information through my own questioning mind and past my heart. I was also very careful to only connect to my Higher Self and the energy of the Holy Spirit. I was still interested in vibrational energy, not for power purposes, but for spiritual growth. Sigi, who had been my ground to reality in India, initiated her own advance, centering on prayer and meditation. Sigi is completely and utterly a heart person. Who else could have put up with everything I had done? We form the perfect balance. I learn from her how to connect to the heart and she learns from me what not to do with the mind. Slowly, we re-established ourselves on the path to spiritual growth.

After the company I partnered with in eastern Germany failed, we made plans to sell everything and move once more back to the United States. I began charting a map of America to see if I could glean any more information about Earth energies. This map was much different from the previous world map, because it represented the emotional body of the Earth (see map 2 at the end of the book). We decided that if we moved to America we wanted to live somewhere warm and on the ocean. With that in mind, we flew to Ft. Meyers, Florida, bought a car in Naples and started driving up the eastern coast of Florida. We wanted to be on the Atlantic and when we drove into St. Augustine, with its 26 miles of sandy beaches, we knew we had found home. Our certainty grew as everything easily fell into place; job, rental house, schools, etc.

The chakra points on my map were apparent by large vortex-like spirals, ending or beginning on a point that came up from or went into the Earth. Some of these vortexes were twinned, like our own chakra system. This means that both ends of a meridian were spiraled. Many lines paralleling each other were packed closely side by side, like conduits or energy highways, which moved off the map heading into Mexico and toward Europe. At two points, one in southern Florida and east of Florida's coast in the Atlantic, many energy lines converged to form a thick bundle, which continued farther south into the Caribbean. The parallel energy lines in the Atlantic also exhibited a large vortex before flowing together. Guidance indicated that this had been a part of the energy constellation of the ancient mythological continent of Atlantis. My attention was directed to a vortex located in northern California, in the Trinity Alps. There was an obvious break in the parallel spiraling of the vortex, which was referred to by guidance as a "chakra rip". I remembered reading in Barbara Brennan's book, Hands of Light, about chakras that could be torn or distorted, which affected the flow of energy (Brennan). It was indicated that I needed to travel there to help bring this energy center back into balance. Fortunately, my brother lived about 40 miles south of the center of this vortex, near Weaverville, California. I had no idea about how I would balance this huge vortex, at that time, but trusted that I would receive the necessary information along the way.

  I took along the Feng Shui Handbook, by Derek Walters, to learn more about what is considered "the Chinese art of placement". Feng Shui deals with the movement of Chi, or Qi, along the land and through man-made structures. Chi is a natural energy force (Yang) that flows in a curving, weaving pattern and is the essential life force. The orientation and position of the home to the type of landscape, the direction of the doorways, positioning of furniture, and even the color and type of room decorations, all become important considerations to retain the maximum amount of Chi in the dwelling. Chi moving in a straight line becomes its opposite, or Sha, which causes sickness and unhappiness by sucking the vitality out of the home. Feng Shui is generally done with the advice of an expert, using an instrument called a Lo Pan. The Feng Shui expert considers all aspects of the energy flow before making recommendations. Areas of the house are given colorful names, such as Six Curses, Celestial Monad, or Severed Fate, indicating its beneficial and detrimental qualities affecting Chi.

The eight directions, north, northeast, southeast, etc., are all represented by a trigram familiar in the I-Ching. The trigram not only stands for the specific direction, but also for the family unit, specific animals, colors, and Earth elemental symbols. For instance, the trigram for northeast is "Kun", the second son, the dragon, the color green, and the element of wood. North is the Kuan trigram (=), the father, the turtle, the color black, the element water, and so on (Walters).

Although interesting, I did not see how this information would be helpful until I arrived in the mountains. I realized, after applying Feng Shui to my brother's house and the surrounding countryside, that the natural features of the land would be an integral part of the balancing of the vortex energy. I also learned the history of the area, which had been heavily mined for gold by masses of Chinese in the preceding century. Tons and tons of gold had been removed and carried to other parts of the world. Gold is considered the master balancer in an aruvedic and vibrational sense. It seemed logical to me, viewing the Earth as an organism, that the removal of huge quantities of gold from these mountains would have caused the imbalance, or tear, in the vortex energy spiral.

Besides the elemental Earth features, Walters also alluded to the 24 star portals, which could be located and integrated into the balancing. We were to make our way to the vortex center and construct a medicine wheel. The wheel should be a circle of stones, ten feet in diameter, aligning the natural features of the Earth with the heavenly star portals.

My brother and I hiked up into the mountains until we located the point indicated by the map, about eight miles from the road. It was situated on a huge rocky projection between two ravines. The view was amazing, with Mt. Shasta to the south, standing tall and snow-covered. We could clearly recognize all of the features in the landscape as presented by Feng Shui. The dragon in the east was clearly discernable, with its tail, back, and head. It was the best possible situation, referred to as "the dragon salivating pearls". This meant that a body of water was at the dragon's mouth, like a mountain lake. Across from the dragon was the white tiger, somewhat indistinct, as it should be, so as to not be too overpowering. North, rising behind us was the black turtle, containing the large round mountain lake. The south opened up to a panoramic view of Mt. Shasta, standing alone in the distance, representing the red bird. We built the medicine wheel, as instructed, and completed the ceremony, arriving back down the mountain as it became dark.

Some months later, I was told by guidance I could further help the Earth by balancing another large vortex located in the Smokey Mountain area, by Asheville, North Carolina. I was not to use a medicine wheel here, but instead, was to use another approach. I had read about the Slovakian, Marko Pogacnik, who sculpted raw granite "needles", inscribing each with a unique symbol he called a "cosmogram". He placed these at energy points in England and northern Germany to balance the Earth's energy. One of his cosmograms was used in the Slovakian national flag. His granite sculptures were works of art, looking mysterious in the hilly English landscape (Pogacnik).

    I received the information that I needed to place a large granite rock directly on the center of the vortex, similar to the stones at Stonehedge, but weighing only about one ton. Wondering how I would ever accomplish this feat, I planned a trip over Christmas vacation to North Carolina to visit my father and my sister's family. I was informed that no tools were necessary and that a suitable granite rock was already near the site.

    On December 22nd, Sigi and I drove north of Asheville to search for the site and plan our strategy. The pendulum led us down a number of back roads into the foothills of the Smokies, until the road stopped and became a trail. We hiked about one mile in a cold drizzling rain, until we came to a plateau nestled between the mountains. There was an old dilapidated barn and an uninhabited one-room cabin nearby. The vortex center was on the edge of a plowed area and exhibited no distinguishing characteristics. We found the designated granite boulder about 20 yards away from the site, downhill.

    My first thought, after trying unsuccessfully to pry up the boulder, was that we needed help. At least several strong people or a tractor would be necessary. We drove back into Asheville to have a coffee, and to contemplate the situation. Friends of ours, living in Asheville, suggested we contact the Asheville Resource Center, run by Mary. We explained to Mary what we wanted to do and showed her our map. She made a call and handed me the phone saying, "This is Fred. Maybe he can help you."

As it turned out, Spirit brought us together with the one person who could solve the problem, but differently than we expected. Fred had developed a procedure he called "gridding". He used a large template to set the pattern for a matrix made of crystals, inserted through various holes in the pattern into the Earth. Fred was excited by the prospect of gridding a major Earth vortex, and we arranged a meeting two days later to do the work. Spirit indicated to me that we should employ this method of balancing and forget the rock, much to my relief.

We met Fred and an energy healer, Rebecca, in a small café in Ashville. I charted their energy, and found that both were surprisingly high frequency, in line with Sigi and myself. After some warm beverages and good conversation, we headed to the point to begin the gridding. Fred had everything prepared perfectly. After spreading out the 14-foot canvas template as smoothly as possible, we oriented it to the compass directions, and fastened it. The pattern on the canvas was a series of shapes consisting of two large infinity symbols, crossing in the middle and oriented to the four compass directions, north, south, east, and west. A large square connected the top of each of the infinity symbols. The proportions of the intersecting lines formed smaller parts that were in accord with what is known as the Phi ratio, or 1 to 1.61803….

Phi is an irrational number whose decimal places go on endlessly, never to be resolved. The Phi ratio has long been recognized in the proportions of the Golden Mean, which is found everywhere in the natural world. On our body, the proportions of the joints to each other are in the Phi ratio, as well as the proportions of the face, the torso, the arms, and legs. With insects, the proportion of the head to the thorax, or the thorax to the abdomen, is in the Phi ratio. The arc of a wave or a whirlpool, traces a pattern corresponding to the Phi ratio. The orbital distance of the planets and the spiral of the DNA strand follow the Phi ratio. The list is endless and indicates a central, unifying pattern to all life.

Fred's patterns of shapes were all drawn to be in exact proportion to the Phi ratio. Besides the two infinity symbols, there were twelve squares, each rotated 90 degrees within the last, getting smaller and smaller toward the middle. Where the lines intersected and at the curvature of the infinity symbols, there were small holes in the template, reinforced by grommets. The effect was to create pathways for energy to flow. Squares represented the masculine energy and the infinity symbols represented the universal energy. The pattern also created a series of spirals, four rotating clockwise, and four counterclockwise, representing the feminine energy. All shapes were balanced in accordance with the Phi ratio.

After spreading and aligning the template, we proceeded to insert small crystals into the ground. Screwdrivers were used to create the holes. We did the work quickly, because it was raining and we were all beginning to get chilled. Fred then linked all of the crystals by tracing the patterns of masculine, feminine, and universal energy. He closed the ceremony, which he called "coning", by thanking all of the unseen participants in the gridding. We collected the template and equipment, but left the crystals in the ground. Fred said that, in his experience, the grid would immediately replicate itself. It would continue to increase in much the same manner as a living fertilized egg, until it expanded to the size of the chakra-vortex.

Compassion

I was well progressed by now, in my ability the chart people's energy. Using the pendulum, I would ask which chakras were open in a twelve-chakra system and what the vibrational frequencies were for both Yin and Yang energies. The yin frequency represents the condition of the physical body and I compare it to the Earth's vibrational frequency. The closer they are to each other, the less likely the person has serious genetic problems and the stronger their immune system seems to be. The frequencies of yang energy give information as to the condition of the energy body. The yang frequency numbers are added together and the higher the total, the fewer energy blockages the person has. I started charting my family and myself initially, to see if I could discover any patterns in the information. As the charting progressed, I began to see correlations in the numbers with the techniques people used for spiritual growth. For example, people who did yoga or meditation had significantly higher numbers than ones who didn't. Reiki healers were very advanced in frequency values. The higher the number of yang units, the fewer blockages and the "lighter" a person was. I saw the charting as a method of quantitatively measuring spiritual growth! At the same time, I realized that it was a hopeless task to quantify Spirit. It was more a visual tool to measure relative growth.

Returning home from Ashville, we each brought the quartz crystal we had used in the gridding ceremony with us. We put them in a small wooden jewelry box at the head of our bed as a memento of our experience. That night, neither of us could sleep at all. We spent the entire night tossing and turning, unable to quiet our minds. I attributed my mental excitement to the fact that I began work again that morning. When the same thing occurred the following night as well, I began searching for another explanation. I checked our energy frequencies and found that there had been a striking increase in the yang frequency values over the past two days. The pendulum indicated that it had something to do with the crystals by our bed. I took the crystals to my office on the other side of the house and we could finally sleep again.

Several days later, I read a book called Earth Energies, which related an experiment the author had performed, concerning energy fields. Using a pendulum, he measured the energy field around a tree-stump that had been hit by lightening fifteen years previously. The pendulum indicated that there was a strong field seven feet in diameter around the stump, becoming weaker out to fourteen feet. His experiment consisted of taking stone containing calcium and placing it on the stump for 24 hours. He then drove 240 miles to his home and put the stone in his yard with a green leaf on top of it. The next day he checked the area with his pendulum and to his amazement, found that the leaf had a force-field exactly the same size and intensity as the stump! He broke up the rock and threw it away, but the energy field had been transferred to the leaf and remained intact. He claimed the leaf stayed green and pliant for the next two years when kept out of direct sunlight (King).

This account opened the possibility that our

crystals had replicated the energy of the grid in North Carolina. I had already noticed a rapid increase in our vibrational frequencies when we were in the proximity of the crystals. If this were true, how could we use this energy matrix to its full potential? The answer came several days later when I received a phone call from Fred. He told me he had sent a grid to us "through the ethers" and that we could anchor it by placing neutral crystals on four sides of our property, aligned with the four directions. I followed his instructions and the pendulum indicated that we had indeed established a weak energy grid around our house. Perhaps by using one of the charged stones, I could increase the vibration of the grid. We placed one in the middle of the existing grid and for the next two nights nobody slept in the house, not even the dog or the cat! It was as if we all had been drinking strong coffee all night. Our energy values continued to climb at an accelerated rate and we noticed that our bodies slowly became accustomed to the change in vibration.

    We also became aware on an additional side effect of the grid. It began to draw large numbers of entities to it. We had already experienced, to some extent, the effect our increased brightness had in attracting entities to us. These entities are spirits that are stuck at this dimensional level and walk in darkness. They are attracted to brightness, as a moth is attracted to light. We found that by calling in help from Christ or the Archangel Michael, we could serve as a bridge to help these spirits to move towards the light. The grid was like a giant bubble of light, which drew in crowds of entities. They wouldn't come into the gridded area, because the frequency was too high, but would hang out around its perimeter instead. For the first few weeks, we had to clear them many times daily, but eventually there were fewer and fewer to clear. The entire area became brighter as more and more of these low frequency souls were directed out.

We discovered that we could load the grid into other crystals by keeping neutral crystals with the crystal containing the grid matrix for twenty-four hours. A neutral crystal was one that had been soaked in a saturated sea salt solution overnight. The newly charged crystal had the same energy field in size and intensity as the original. This made it possible to load multiple crystals and establish additional grids for other people. Whenever we set up another grid, however, we were always careful to mention the phenomena of the entities and give instructions on clearing them.

In February we were given the assignment to grid a large chakra-vortex in southern Florida. Its center was in Frostproof, Florida, and it extended all the way to Miami and West Palm Beach. This chakra also had a "rip", like the chakra in northern California and again in Asheville, which was evident in its irregular spiraling energy lines. The date was set for February 22, 1999, or numerological, 2221999. "Coincidentally", at this point, we met Kin, Eileen and their baby Coral at a garage sale. Kin was a young man in his mid-twenties and was from Frostpoof. He offered to accompany us there and help in any way he could. It was the beginning of a long friendship.

Fred drove down from Asheville to be our Master of Ceremony. He brought a new template with him. It was similar to the previous one, but was measured more precisely and lay closer to the ground. It also had thirteen squares in its center instead of twelve to further expand consciousness.

Compassion

We arrived in Frostproof early that afternoon, but to our surprise, a little league baseball game was in progress on the adjacent property. It was impossible to do anything unobtrusively for the moment. We needed to wait until everyone departed before we could begin. Kin's parents still lived in town, so we paid them a visit and were treated to a delicious meal. As it became dark, we drove back and found the area deserted.

Our daughters are able to see into the spiritual realm. They told us that the entire area was packed with angels, Archangels, and hundreds of other spiritual beings, which had come to support us. We conducted the gridding ceremony, after which, the assembly of esteemed guests disbanded.

As the grid expanded, an increasing number of people began calling me from the Miami area. I drove down several times to give lectures to people interested in my method of charting and my experiences. Juanita, a Reiki Master and Reiki teacher sponsored some of these talks. People began calling me from all over the United States and sending me E-mail to obtain charts and energy readings. Someone always referred them to me, but all had one thing in common: The desire to grow spiritually.

That summer, we were directed to travel to New Mexico to work on the heart chakra of the Earth. I was already aware from my previous map, that the heart of the Earth is located in an area including southern California, Arizona, New Mexico, Colorado and southern Nevada. The heart chakra is to be found in northern New Mexico, near the Four Corners. The chakra-vortex there, according to my map, was very distorted, looking more like a spiral crescent than a spiral circle. It was in the middle of the Hopi Indian area. We decided to make it a family effort and drove there in our van.

Sightseeing and camping along the way, we finally arrived in late July. The center of the chakra was off the main highway about five miles on someone's private property. We had always been fortunate to find the points either on public property or at least not within the sight of residences, until now. This time, however, we had to cross two sets of barbed wire, several fields and a stream, all in plain sight to neighboring farmhouses. Somehow we managed to reach the prescribed point without alerting anyone. We did the work we needed to do and were rewarded by the cries of nearby coyotes as they thanked us.

Since then, we have balanced several vortex areas in Florida, including Orlando, the Tampa-St. Petersburg area and the Naples-Ft. Meyers area. Initially, I thought that our work contributed towards the tremendous increase in frequency that the Earth was undergoing. I later realized that the Earth is involved in its own evolution and we are providing support in its release by balancing and repairing its chakra system. This allows the Earth to release in a way that is less disastrous for its inhabitants. There is still much work to do, especially on other continents, but the heart chakra is open and clear, and that is the first step!

Case Histories

Case History 1

This chart was one of the more unusual cases. I acquired permission to do the chart from the girl's father through a friend of the father. I did her chart and then later the father's. I had never seen a chart like this girl's before and was interested afterwards to find out more about her. I was told that both she and her father lived in Brazil, but that she had been institutionalized as a paranoid schizophrenic. She was an intuitive and directed an uncommonly large percentage of her energy through her heart chakra, 20%. Her yang frequency was also very high, already over the threshold of 22,200 units. The consciousness level, or ray, was low for her frequency, indicating a major blockage. The problem was the spiritual blockage, which always points to an attachment or possession from an entity. I cleared the entity for her, but received no further information as to the outcome.

Date: 10/31/1999
Sex: Female (21 years old)

Blockage: yes
Gift: intuitive
Unit: no

Chart 1

Yin	Chakra	%	Yang	Ray
	12			Emerald
0	11	0	5157	Diamond
0	10	0	4574	Platinum
207	9	0	3963	Gold
207	8	9	3285	White
207	7	13	2657	Indigo
206	6	12	2024	Violet
206	5	8	1583	Blue
206	4	20	1078	Green
206	3	13	676	Yellow
205	2	13	369	Orange
205	1	12	12	Red
	Total	100	25,378	

Comments: Blockage in the spiritual body

Case History 2

The father also had a problem in the spiritual body, but a misalignment problem instead of a blockage. Although spiritual body problems are rare, when I do occasionally come across one, there is often a close friend or family member with a similar problem. People with strong karmic connections tend to travel through lifetimes together. Both of their heart chakras were open and clear, which is also unusual for adults. The N/A means the he has no primary way he perceives the world, but instead distributes his energy in a more or less even fashion through the chakras.

Date: 11/8/1999
Sex: Male (father of girl)

Blockage: yes
Gift: N/A
Unit: no

Chart 2

Yin	Chakra	%	Yang	Ray
	12			Emerald
	11	0	2847	Diamond
	10	0	2453	Platinum
	9	8	1992	Gold
	8	8	1548	White
	7	13	1157	Indigo
⋈	6	12	767	Violet
	5	8	563	Blue
	4	13	383	Green
	3	13	224	Yellow
	2	13	111	Orange
	1	12	12	Red
	Total	100	12,057	

Comments: Misalignment of the spiritual body

Case History 3

This man is a visionary, meaning he directs a larger percentage of his energy through his 6th and 7th chakras. He had numerous major blockages and a misalignment. Interesting in this chart is the yang blockage in the emotional body at the 3rd chakra. He brought it in with him as a karmic pattern. If a man has a major yang energy blockage, it means he has difficulty dealing with that energy. He tends to seek a partner, another man, that will allow him to call up those blockages so that he can resolve them. He also has yin blockage and in our conversation afterwards, he told me he was bi-sexual.

Date: 10/29/00
Sex: Male

Blockage: yes
Gift: visionary
Unit: no

Chart 3

Yin	Chakra	%	Yang	Ray
	12			Emerald
	11			Diamond
0	<u>10</u>	0	538	Platinum
220	<u>9</u>	2	476	Gold
219	<u>8</u>	9	417	White
218	<u>7</u>	16	358	Indigo
217	<u>6</u>	14	299	Violet
216	<u>5</u>	9	238	<u>Blue</u>
215	<u>4</u>	12	176	Green
214	<u>3</u>	13	115	Yellow
213	<u>2</u>	13	56	Orange
212	<u>1</u>	12	12	Red
	Total	100	2685	

Comments: Heart blocked; Yang blockage in the emotional body at the 3rd chakra; Yin blockage in the mental body; misalignment of the mental body

Case History 4

This woman has the most extensive blockages and misalignments I have ever encountered. Every subtle body is misaligned. Her gift is that of a prophet, meaning she directs a higher percentage of her energy through her fourth and seventh chakras. Normally, this would be an advantageous configuration, providing a balance between heart and mind. In her case, however, it doesn't really matter. Many of her major problems are karmic, including her yang blockage of the emotional body, the misalignment of the mental body and the spiritual body misalignment. She has reoccurring memories of a past life that seem as real and vivid to her as her present life memories.

Date: 11/7/00
Sex: Female

Blockage: yes
Gift: prophet
Unit: no

Chart 4

Yin	Chakra	%	Yang	Ray
	12			Emerald
	11			Diamond
	10			Platinum
216	<u>9</u>	2	652	Gold
216	<u>8</u>	8	569	White
216	<u>7</u>	16	487	Indigo
215	<u>6</u>	11	403	Violet
214	<u>5</u>	9	327	<u>Blue</u>
213	<u>4</u>	16	240	Green
212	<u>3</u>	13	158	Yellow
211	<u>2</u>	13	76	Orange
210	<u>1</u>	12	12	Red
	Total	100	2924	

Comments: Heart blockage; Yang blockage in the emotional body; misalignment of the emotional body; misalignment of the mental body; misalignment of the spiritual body

Case History 5

In this chart, we again see an intuitive. This means she processes the world mostly at a heart level. The blockages for an intuitive tend to be heart and emotion oriented. She also has formed a unit with a partner, or a soul contract, which means that their energies are merged and move together. When advising a person in a unit, it is necessary to work on both people.

Date: 10/15/00
Sex: Female

Blockage: yes
Gift: intuitive
Unit: yes

Chart 5

Yin	Chakra	%	Yang	Ray
	12			Emerald
	11			Diamond
0	<u>10</u>	0	944	Platinum
220	<u>9</u>	5	840	Gold
219	<u>8</u>	9	736	White
218	<u>7</u>	12	631	Indigo
217	<u>6</u>	11	527	<u>Violet</u>
216	<u>5</u>	9	422	Blue
215	<u>4</u>	16	316	Green
214	<u>3</u>	13	210	Yellow
213	<u>2</u>	13	102	Orange
212	<u>1</u>	12	12	Red
	Total	100	4740	

Comments: Heart blockage; Yang blockage in the emotional body; misalignment of the emotional body; misalignment of the spiritual body

Case History 6

This young man is serving time in jail for a sex related crime. The blockage and the misalignment of the emotional body are karmic. The blockage in the spiritual body indicates an attachment by a low frequency entity. These entities try to release their own negative karma through their hosts. It is my guess that the jails and asylums are full of situations like this.

Date: 3/7/00
Sex: Male

Blockage: yes
Gift: N/A
Unit: no

Chart 6

Yin	Chakra	%	Yang	Ray
	12			Emerald
	11			Diamond
	10	0		Platinum
209	9	7	186	Gold
208	8	9	158	White
207	7	13	137	Indigo
206	6	12	110	Violet
205	5	9	92	Blue
205	4	12	69	Green
204	3	13	46	Yellow
203	2	13	26	Orange
202	1	12	12	Red
	Total	100	836	

Comments: Heart blockage; Yin blockage in the emotional body; misalignment of the emotional body; blockage in the spiritual body

Case History 7

This is how most babies come into the world. I began charting this baby still in its mother's womb. Newborns have not yet formed a pattern for perceiving the world and are therefore all N/A. Their entry-level energy is also generally well above 22,200 yang units. This baby is bringing in Yin blockage patterned into its astral body, where most karmic patterns are stored between lifetimes.

Date: 12/29/1999
Sex: Male (baby)

Blockage: no
Gift: N/A
Unit: no

Chart 7

Yin	Chakra	%	Yang	Ray
	<u>12</u>	0	4278	Emerald
	<u>11</u>	0	3775	Diamond
	<u>10</u>	0	3247	Platinum
	<u>9</u>	10	2692	Gold
	<u>8</u>	8	2239	White
	<u>7</u>	13	1868	Indigo
⧖	<u>6</u>	12	1483	<u>Violet</u>
	<u>5</u>	8	1074	Blue
	<u>4</u>	14	888	Green
	<u>3</u>	12	576	Yellow
	<u>2</u>	12	265	Orange
	<u>1</u>	11	11	Red
	Total	100	22,200+	

Comments: Yin blockage

Case History 8

This boy is severely handicapped, both mentally and physically. The father attributes it to possible ineptitude of the delivering doctor, but I believe it was this soul's own choice. There are no major blockages here to remove or subtle bodies to realign. The frequencies for yin energy in the first and second chakra are very low compared to the rest, indicating extreme physical problems. He came in on a high consciousness ray, indigo, which indicates he had already evolved to a high state in his previous lifetime. His is a mission to teach compassion. Occasionally a soul will choose to enter a lifetime with a severe disability to resolve a huge portion of their karma and to teach compassion and unconditional love to those around them. This boy is such a great soul.

Date: 11/21/00
Sex: Male

Blockage: yes
Gift: N/A
Unit: no

Chart 8

Yin	Chakra	%	Yang	Ray
	12			Emerald
	11			Diamond
	10			Platinum
215	<u>9</u>	4	297	Gold
214	<u>8</u>	9	261	White
213	<u>7</u>	12	222	<u>Indigo</u>
212	<u>6</u>	11	186	Violet
212	<u>5</u>	9	148	Blue
211	<u>4</u>	16	112	Green
210	<u>3</u>	13	77	Yellow
58	<u>2</u>	12	35	Orange
57	<u>1</u>	14	16	Red
	Total	100	1354	

Comments: no major blockage

Energetic Awakening

Case History 9

This man is a feeler, as I am. This means that his primary perception of the world is through his mind. Feelers are generally very egocentric and often have difficulty connecting to the heart. Blockage or misalignments for a feeler are usually in the mental body. He also has formed a unit with his wife. A unit forms only with opposite sexed partners. Divorce does not necessarily break the unit, because it is a contract at a soul level. Only the Higher Self can make that choice.

Date: 10/25/1999
Sex: Male

Blockage: yes
Gift: feeler
Unit: yes

Chart 9

Yin	Chakra	%	Yang	Ray
	12			Emerald
	11			Diamond
	10			Platinum
188	9	6	96	Gold
188	8	7	78	White
187	7	17	66	Indigo
187	6	11	56	Violet
187	5	8	42	Blue
186	4	13	31	Green
186	3	13	25	Yellow
185	2	13	16	Orange
185	1	12	12	Red
	Total	100	422	

Comments: Heart chakra blockage; Yin blockage in the mental body; misalignment of the mental body

Energetic Awakening

Map 1

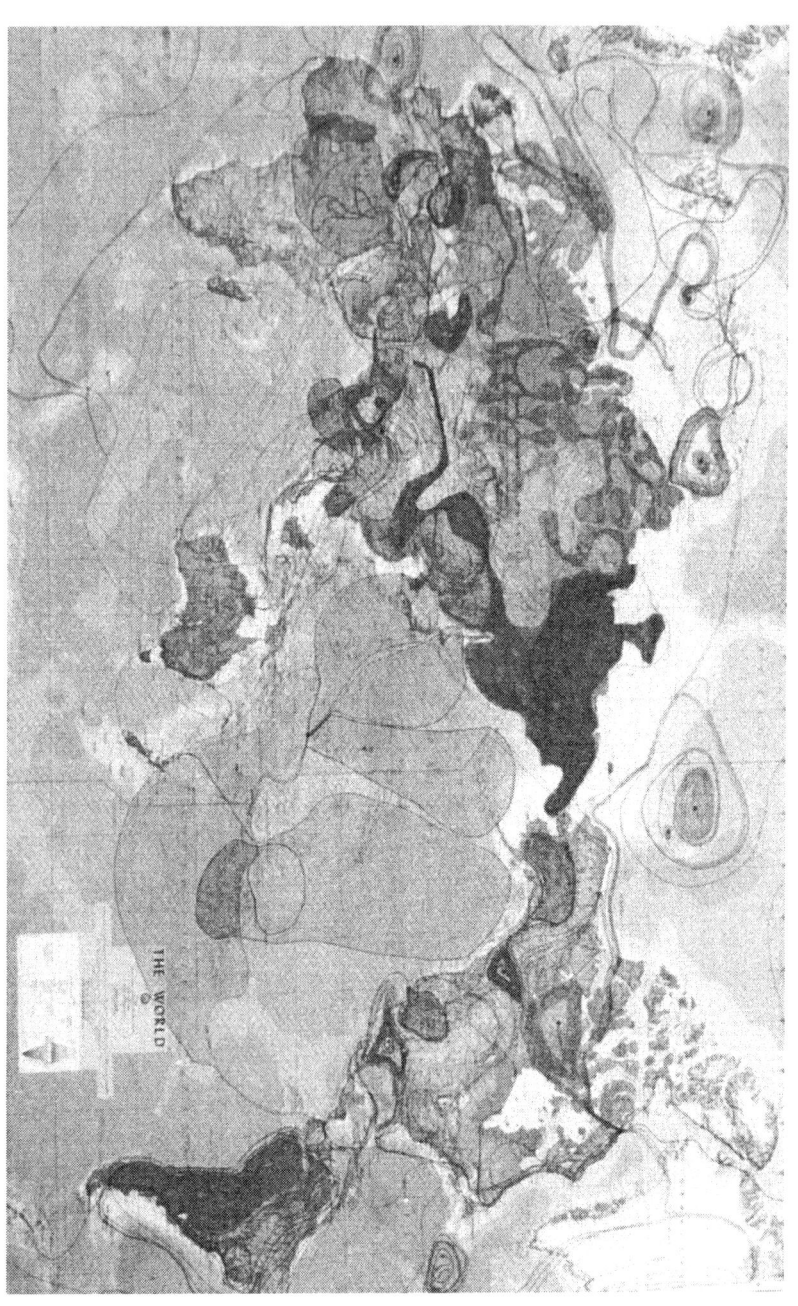

Organs of the Earth

Map 2

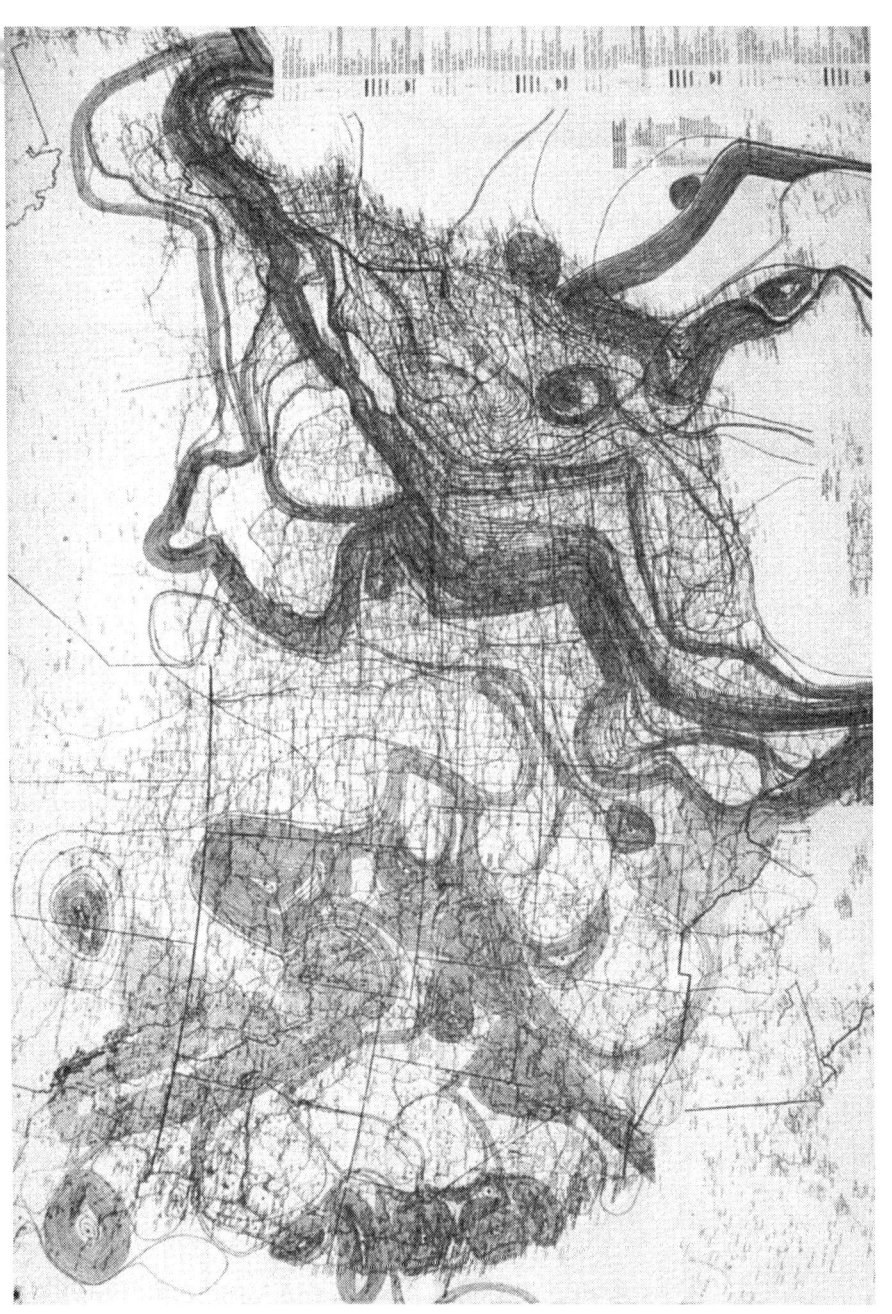

Energy Body of the UnitedStates

Bibliography

Brennan, Barbara Ann, Hands of Light, Bantam Books, 1988.

Foundation For Inner Peace, A Course in Miracles, Viking Penguin, 1996 revised.

King, Serge Kahili, Earth Energies, The Theosophical Publishing House, Wheaten, Ill., 1992.

Leonhardt, Horst, M.D., Fundamentals of Electroacupuncture According to Voll, Medizinisch Literarische Verlagsgesellschaft mbH, Uelzen, Germany, 1980.

McIntosh, Stephen Ian, The Golden Mean Book & Caliper Set, Now & Zen, Inc., Boulder, Colorado, 1997.

Myss, Caroline, Ph.D., Anatomy of the Spirit, Three Rivers Press, New York, NY, 1996.

Pogacnik, Marko, Die Landschaft der Goettin, Eugen Diederichs Verlag, Munich, Germany, 1993.

Talbot, Michael, The Holographic Universe, HarperCollins Publishers, New York, NY, 1992.

Walters, Derek, The Feng Shui Handbook, Thorsons, San Francisco, California, 1995.